Tantric Practice in Nying-ma

Tantric Practice in Nying-ma

Khetsun Sangpo Rinbochay

TRANSLATED AND EDITED BY
Jeffrey Hopkins
Co-edited by Anne C. Klein

Snow Lion
Boston & London

Snow Lion
An imprint of Shambhala Publications, Inc.
Horticultural Hall
300 Massachusetts Avenue
Boston, Massachusetts 02115
www.shambhala.com

Printed in the United States of America

Distributed in the United States by Penguin Random House LLC
and in Canada by Random House of Canada Ltd

Library of Congress Cataloging-in-Publication Data
Khetsun Sangpo Rinbochay.
Tantric Practice in Nying-ma.
Includes bibliographical references and index.
ISBN 978-0-937938-14-0 (pbk.)
1. Rñiṅ-ma-pa (Sect)—Doctrines. 2. Spiritual life (Buddhism)—
Rñiṅ-ma-pa authors. 3. Tantric Buddhism—China—Tibet.
I. Hopkins, Jeffrey. II. Klein, Anne. III. Title.
[BQ7662.4.K47 1986]
294.3'4448
86-3762

Contents

6 *Contents*

Preface

Khetsun Sangpo Rinbochay is a Nying-ma lama trained in Tibet and capable of transmitting in complete form the special precepts of Nying-ma (Old Translation Order). Student of the Ge-luk, Sa-gya, Ga-gyu, and Nying-ma orders while in Tibet, member of the lay clergy whose many functions included the stopping of hail to protect crops, teacher in Japan for ten years at the request of His Holiness the Dalai Lama, and author of an eight-volume series of biographies of Tibetan masters, Khetsun Sangpo Rinbochay came to the University of Virginia in the spring of 1974 to lecture on tantric Buddhism. In a series of lectures, during which I acted as his translator, he set forth the prerequisite practices for tantra, beginning with instructions on how to listen to religious teaching and ending with guru yoga.

During Rinbochay's visit to America in 1974 and my visit to India in 1972, I was fortunate to receive his teaching on Long-chen-rap-jam's presentation of the nine vehicles in his *Treasury of the Supreme Vehicle (Theg mchog mdzod)*,[1] the same author's presentation of the sutra system in his *Treasury of Tenets (Grub mtha' mdzod)*, and Ba-drul Jik-may-chö-gi-wang-bo's *Sacred Word of Lama Gun-sang (Kun bzang bla ma'i zhal lung)* – Rinbochay's condensation of which forms the basis for this book. In the light of his teaching and of a twentieth-century commentary on the

Sacred Word of Lama Gun-sang by Nga-wang-bel-sang, I collaborated with Anne Klein to edit Rinbochay's lectures on the *Sacred Word of Lama Gun-sang* and other teachings on the Great Perfection.

These provide the classical Nying-ma presentation of the preparatory tantric paths as well as a glimpse into the higher reaches of tantric realization. Khetsun Sangpo Rinbochay's transmission of the oral tradition vividly reveals the practicality that is at the root of all religious endeavour.

JEFFREY HOPKINS
Charlottesville, Virginia

Technical Note

The transliteration scheme for Sanskrit names and titles is aimed at easy pronunciation, using *sh*, *sh*, and *ch* rather than *ś*, *s*, and *c*. With the first occurrence of each Indian title, the Sanskrit is given, if available. The full Sanskrit and Tibetan titles are to be found in the bibliography, which is arranged alphabetically according to the English titles of sutras and according to authors of other works. The Tibetan originals of key terms have been given in a glossary at the end.

Turrell Wylie's presentation of a transliteration scheme for the Tibetan alphabet[2] has been followed (except in that root letters are capitalized in names). For an explanation of the rendering of Tibetan names in a pronounceable form see the technical note to *Meditation on Emptiness*.[3]

PART ONE

Common External Preparatory Practices

Khetsun Sangpo Rinbochay's commentary on the first part of *The Sacred Word of Lama Gun-sang*, also known as *Instructions on the Preliminaries to the Great Perfection Teaching Called 'Heart Essence of Vast Openness,' the Sacred Word of Lama Gun-sang*

1 Introduction

The *Instructions on the Preliminaries to the Great Perfection Teaching Called 'Heart Essence of Vast Openness', the Sacred Word of Lama Gun-sang*, was written by Ba-drul Jik-may-chö-gi-wang-bo (*dPal-sprul 'Jigs-med-chos-kyi-dbang-po*, born 1808). Each word in his title is meaningful. 'Perfection' (*rDzogs*) means that there is no higher practice. It refers to the perfection of the five paths and ten grounds of the Mahayana and suggests all the auspicious qualities of the Buddhas and Bodhisattvas.

'Great' (*Chen*) means that there is no greater or more expansive teaching. It signifies that this teaching belongs to the Mahayana (Great Vehicle) and not the Hinayana (Lesser Vehicle). The Mahayana has two types of paths, sutra and tantra. The Great Perfection (*rDzogs-chen*) teaches both, but is itself included within the tantric path. It contains the full meaning of all sutras and tantras.

What does 'Vast Openness' (*kLong-chen*) mean? This is the openness (*kLong*) of thought of the Truth Body (*Dharmakāya*) as well as of all Conqueror Buddhas. Because its extent is limitless, it is called great or vast (*chen*).

The thought of Buddha has three forms, that of the Truth Body, the Complete Enjoyment Body (*Saṃbhogakāya*) and the Emanation Body (*Nirmāṇakāya*).

The Truth Body is the body of emptiness that is beyond all elaborations of thought, the ultimate truth fully realized.

How is this? The Truth Body, which is the nature of Peace, has passed beyond all conceptions of object and subject; it is a state of having extinguished all elaborations of thought, and from its essence the Body of Complete Enjoyment arises. The Truth Body is like a clear glass, and the light coming from it is the Complete Enjoyment Body, a pure, eternal manifestation in form of the highest truth. Emanations from the Complete Enjoyment Body manifest in any form necessary to tame and help sentient beings. Each is an instance of an Emanation Body.

There are special female deities known as Mothers and Sky Goers for whom this teaching is as precious as the essence of their own heart. To those who cherish it, it is known as the 'Heart Essence' (*sNying thig*).

The preliminaries taught here are of two types: common external and special internal preparations. Both are prerequisite practices for final teaching in accordance with the doctrine of the Great Perfection.

At the end of this long title, there is a shorter secondary one, '*The Sacred Word of Lama Gun-sang.*' He was the lama of the author, Ba-drul Jik-may-chö-gi-wang-bo, who wrote the book based on his teacher's lectures. 'Sacred Word' means the unmistaken word that Lama Gun-sang spoke to him.

Before beginning the actual text, the author makes an obeisance, saying:[4]

I bow down to the glorious lamas having great inconceivable compassion.

What does 'inconceivable' mean? It is the inconceivability of subject and object. This compassionate mind does not conceive of subject and object; it does not posit inherent existence (*svabhāva-siddhi*) to an external object. A being with this compassion does not think that an inherently existent external object is cognized by an inherently existent internal mind. Is this 'inconceivable', which is a negative expression, a sign of nihilism? Not at all. The negative indicates that the ordinary type of mind cannot conceive such compassion. Ba-drul Rin-bo-chay [the Precious Ba-drul] is paying obeisance to lamas who have this compassion, and he calls them 'glorious'.[5]

'Glorious' also refers to the glory of Lama Gun-sang himself, who freed himself from cyclic existence (*saṃsāra*) so that there is no chance of his ever suffering again. It also refers to his glory with regard to others – his compassion for those still in cyclic existence. The lama's special realization or mode of cognition prevents him from falling into cyclic existence.

There are two types of realization, visionary and cognitive, and within the visionary there are many different types. Here we will talk mainly about the visions of appearance, emptiness, and bliss.[6]

Just as there are many different objects that appear to our eye consciousness, so there are many objects that appear to our mental consciousness. These are visions of appearance. The factor of objects appearing to a consciousness without an inherently existent subject and object being posited is the vision of emptiness. When the vision of emptiness – the absence of the signs of subject and object – is seen, a bliss is generated within the person, and this is the vision of bliss. Ba-drul Rin-bo-chay bows down to the glorious lamas who have all these qualities.

He also pays homage to the Nying-ma transmissions:

> I bow down to the lamas of the three transmissions, those through the Conqueror's thought, through the symbols of Knowledge Bearers [and through persons' ears]. Their fortune far surpassing that of other people, they were sustained by the excellent and perfected their own and others' welfare.

Lama Gun-sang belongs to the Nying-ma order of Tibetan Buddhism. This has three transmissions, through the Conqueror's thought, the symbols of Knowledge Bearers, and ears. The transmission through the Conqueror's thought passes directly from the Complete Enjoyment Body, the pure eternal manifestation of the truth, to the trainee. This is a case of mental transmission where one being transmits his thought to another directly without words and symbols. The Complete Enjoyment Body, which in this case is Samantabhadra, transfers whatever he knows directly to the minds of his students. Disciples who appear directly to a Buddha can receive such instruction.

The second transmission is through the symbols of Knowledge Bearers. When thought cannot be directly transmitted, it is necessary to depend on symbols. For example, at a crossroad there are signs indicating directions; through seeing them you know where to go. There are no words involved, you understand them through certain arrangements of colour and shape. Vajradhara himself transmitted understanding to his students by using signs and symbols. He originated this transmission, and five different types of beings – gods, dragons, demons, *lichavis*, and *yakṣhas* – passed on the transmission after receiving it from him. Knowledge Bearers, those who bear knowledge of suchness in their minds, transmit this tradition. Knowledge of suchness, the immutable nature of all objects, is the means to escape from cyclic existence; without this knowledge you are trapped.

For those who cannot understand the teaching transmitted through signs and symbols there is a transmission through ears. Here the teacher's thought is expressed in words which enter the ear. How is the teaching done? One way is through empowering blessings, another through hearing scriptures, and a third through initiation. In dependence on such transmission, one engages in practice and actualizes the truth.

Ba-drul Rin-bo-chay next bows down to Long-chen-rap-jam (*kLong-chen-rab-'byams*), a great Nying-ma master:

> I bow down to the omniscient king of doctrine [Long-chen-rap-jam] who gained the thought of the Truth Body in the sphere of extinguishment of phenomena, who saw the pure land of the Enjoyment Body appear in the sphere of clear light, and who aids the welfare of living beings by showing Emanation Bodies to trainees.

Long-chen-rap-jam understood the Truth Body in the sphere of extinguishment which is the nature of phenomena. This refers to the gradual extinguishment of conceptuality within one's own mind. Like a fire burning fuel, the mind consumes conception by working with it. Long-chen-rap-jam understood this sphere of extinguishment which is the final nature of objects.

The homage also refers to seeing the appearance of the pure land of the Enjoyment Body in the sphere of clear light. What is clear light? It is the substance of our dreams and visions. At first it is difficult to meditate on the clear light of sleep or dream because you find it hard to dream. But gradually you learn to increase dreaming. When a yogi does this, he increases his dreams to the point where he has them even before falling asleep. Then his dreaming gradually decreases, and finally the whole process turns into an experience of something like empty space. At that time it is possible for a very special mind endowed with bliss, clarity and non-conceptuality to appear from within. If you are able to cause this clear light to shine, you can know the minds of others.

If such practices and attainments exist, then why are there not many clairvoyants and mind-readers? Too many people spend their time on worldly affairs and do not meditate enough. However, if the activities of this life are laid aside and effort is directed toward meditation, one can develop many wonderful qualities. Long-chen-rap-jam attained the clear light and in it was able to see the pure lands of the Enjoyment Bodies.

An Enjoyment Body has five definite features, those of teacher, retinue, doctrine, time and place. The explanation of these five features is very difficult to believe. The first definite quality is the *teacher*, who is the Enjoyment Body himself and who lasts forever. The *retinue* consists only of tenth-ground Bodhisattvas. The *doctrine* is that of the wordless Mahayana, which is taught continuously by the Enjoyment Body that never needs to rest. The *time* indicates that the wheel of teaching never stops turning.

The *place* is the Highest Pure Land (*Akaniṣhṭha*). Bā-drul Rin-bo-chay makes a third obeisance:

> I bow down to the Knowledge Bearer Jik-may-ling-ba ['Jigs-med-gling-pa] who sees with wisdom the suchness of all that can be known, whose rays of compassion shine for the glory of trainees, and who illumines the teaching of the highest vehicle, the profound path.

Jik-may-ling-ba sees with wisdom the suchness of all existents; he knows all objects of knowledge – all things, from forms through to omniscient consciousnesses. What does it mean to see their suchness? He sees the final nature – emptiness – of each and every one of these phenomena which remains such unchangeably whether or not it is taught and realized. His compassion is like the sun; its rays enter his disciples and help them. He also illumines the teaching of the highest vehicle, the practices of the profound path.

According to the Nying-ma system there are nine vehicles. A vehicle is a system of practice by which one progresses to a higher state. The nine vehicles are arranged into three groups of three. The three external ones leading away from the source of cyclic existence are those of Hearers, Solitary Realizers and Bodhisattvas. The three inner ones involving all types of asceticism are the three lower tantras: Action, Performance and Yoga (*Kriyā, Charyā, Yoga*). The three secret vehicles serving as methods of empowerment are Mahayoga, Anuyoga, Atiyoga. Bā-drul Rin-bo-chay pays homage to Jik-may-ling-ba who illumined Atiyoga, the highest of all systems of practice for developing the mind.

In a final obeisance he bows down to his own teacher, who was the incarnation of the deity Avalokiteshvara. He says:

> I bow down to my kind fundamental lama [Padma Gun-sang] the deity Avalokiteshvara who assumed the ways of a teacher and through the sport of his speech set on the path of liberation all who were related to him. His activities appropriate for all trainees are infinite.

Why did Ba-drul Rin-bo-chay pay homage to his lineage? He praises them in order to receive empowerment from the Buddhas in the form of blessings so that he will not be interrupted while writing his book. He shows that it is important to praise the Buddhas before engaging in virtuous activity.

After his obeisance, he promises to compose the book:

> In accordance with my ascertainment of the errorless word of my unparalleled Lama [Gun-sang], I will explain clearly in terms easy to understand the amazingly profound meaning, the complete teaching, the books of the omniscient transmission, the pith of quintessential instructions, the doctrine for complete enlightenment in one lifetime. I will explain the common external and uncommon internal preparations for the path.... May the lamas and gods empower me to do so.

Buddha's teaching is of two types, verbal and realized. The former consists of words detailing excellent qualities of mind and practices for attaining them. The latter are realizations attained through following the verbal teaching just as it is. Therefore, the actual teaching of Buddha is identified as these two, whereas books and common teachers whom you can meet are just conventional instructors.

When Ba-drul Rin-bo-chay says that he will explain the complete teaching, he means that he will cover all nine vehicles. He will explain the books of the omniscient transmission, a lineage that includes all the famous lamas whom he has just mentioned. He will reveal the pith of quintessential instructions, doctrines by which a person in one lifetime, with his or her ordinary body, can attain complete Buddhahood.

The path to Buddhahood has two parts, preparatory and actual. There are two types of preparation: common external and special internal. These will be explained clearly and simply, and the meaning will be amazingly profound.

2 Motivation

The six common external preparations are meditations on
(i) the difficulty of attaining opportunities and conditions,
(ii) the impermanence of life, (iii) the faults of cyclic
existence, (iv) the causes and effects of actions, (v) the
benefits of liberation, and (vi) reliance on a spiritual friend.[7]

Instruction on the difficulty of acquiring opportunities
and conditions begins with advice on the motivation for
listening to the teaching. A Bodhisattva's motivation is
known as an altruistic mind of enlightenment with vast
thought. Let me explain this.

We use the term cyclic existence to describe our type of
life because we pass from one existence to another like links
on a chain. Cyclic existence is beginningless; all sentient
beings including yourself have been wandering from life to
life since time without beginning. There is no one who has
not been your mother or father on some occasion in the
past. When as a newborn child – the son or daughter of any
of these beings – you were unable to eat unaided, they
sustained you with food. They took care of you from the
time you were a tiny child until you were an adult. They
gave you the very best and newest clothes. They looked
after you, not with weak but very strong and dedicated
love. Each and every sentient being has done this for you,
and thus any living being you see is someone who has been
very kind to you in the past. It is important to think about as

many different types of sentient beings as you can and to reflect on their closeness and kindness to you.

What do all these beings want? They want what is good and satisfying, in short, happiness. If beings knew how to create happiness, they would indeed soon achieve it. However, the fact is that although they want happiness, they do not know its causes and so cannot effect their own wish.

What are the causes of happiness? We can enumerate them as the ten virtues:

Three physical virtues
    abandoning killing and sustaining life
    abandoning stealing and engaging in giving
    abandoning sexual misconduct and maintaining pure ethics
Four verbal virtues
    abandoning lying and speaking the truth
    abandoning divisiveness and speaking harmoniously
    abandoning harsh words and speaking lovingly
    abandoning senseless talk and talking sensibly
Three mental virtues
    abandoning covetousness and cultivating joy for others' prosperity
    abandoning harmful thoughts and cultivating helpfulness
    abandoning wrong ideas and learning correct views.

The opposites are the ten non-virtues, which cause suffering: the three physical non-virtues of killing, stealing, and sexual misconduct; the four verbal non-virtues of lying, divisiveness, harmful speech and senseless talk; the three mental non-virtues of covetousness, harmfulness and wrong views. Because sentient beings want happiness but engage in the ten non-virtues which cause suffering, their wishes and actions are at cross-purposes.

You should practise the ten virtues for the sake of all sentient beings. The wish to help them all should be cultivated so that it motivates you to listen to and practise doctrine. You should practise virtue in order to be able to help others to do so, thereby making them happy. Highest enlightenment should be sought for the sake of freeing all sentient beings, and such altruism should be cherished whenever you hear or teach the doctrine.

The distinguishing feature of the Mahayana path is that all virtuous activity is accompanied by altruistic motivation. Whether you are listening to, thinking about, or actually achieving doctrine, your activity must be preceded and sustained by an attitude intent on the welfare of others. Whether your activity is little or great, it can never be Mahayana practice unless it is accompanied by altruism.

All practice should include the three excellences. The first occurs prior to a practice and consists of ascertaining why it should be done. One determines that it is for the sake of all suffering sentient beings in the world systems.

The second excellence consists of acting without conceiving the inherent existence of agent, action, and object. Whenever we practise with our ordinary consciousness, we think that each agent, action, and object of the deed exists inherently, in and of itself, and has its own mode of being. In this way we misconceive the nature of agent, action, and object. This pollutes even virtue with a sense of inherent existence and makes it possible for virtue to be ruined by circumstances that cause anger or desire to arise during the practice. Because such afflictions depend on a conception of inherent existence, it is important to understand the non-inherent existence of the virtuous agent, action, and object when practising virtue.

The third excellence is the final sealing of the action through dedicating it to the welfare of all sentient beings. This not only increases the virtue but also prevents it from being destroyed. If virtuous activity is not dedicated after completion, its value can be lost through anger. Therefore, at the end of a session the merit should be dedicated to the welfare of all sentient beings, whereby it becomes related with a limitless field of beings and is thus so powerful that it cannot be destroyed.

Let us illustrate the three excellences by applying them to your hearing of religious practice and to my explanation. If you think that you are listening to this not for your own sake, but for that of every being throughout the world systems, then you have the first excellence. Similarly, if my motive in explaining religious practice is, 'May this help all sentient beings,' I will have the first excellence.

Not to conceive agent, action and object as inherently existent is the second excellence. For a listener this means that with undistracted attention to what is said you analyse and then understand that the listener, listening and listened lack inherent existence. For my part, if I explain the topics correctly without confusing the order and also analyse the explainer, explaining and explained, I will have the second excellence.

The third excellence is to dedicate whatever virtue you have achieved. Instead of jumping up after a lecture and rushing off to whatever is next, you should take a moment to reflect, 'May whatever virtue there has been in listening to religious practice be dedicated to the welfare of all sentient beings.' Similarly before leaving I would reflect, 'Through the virtue of explaining religious practice here, may all throughout space attain omniscience.'

Dedications such as these are not to be confused with prayer-petitions. Dedication occurs after doing a virtuous act, whereas a prayer-petition is the expression of a wish so to act. For instance, the thought, 'May I be able to aspire to highest enlightenment,' is a prayer-petition. Through these petitions and dedications the field of relation of the deed is no longer your own mind but all sentient beings throughout space. When prayer precedes and dedication follows virtuous activity, it is like placing gold or silver in the care of a trustworthy person. It will not be lost.

It is initially important to know how to hear — for example, how to pay proper physical respect to the teaching

– but mental motivation is even more important. For example, a Bodhisattva in India realized clairvoyantly that a boatman was intending to kill five hundred Arhats. In order to prevent him from doing what would bring him great suffering in the future, the Bodhisattva killed him and so achieved merit that would normally take seventy thousand aeons to accumulate. It appeared not to be a virtue but it was.

There is another story of a merchant who bought many religious books. However, his intention was not to spread the practices but to win fame for himself. A poor old lady saw him with his books and, not knowing his motives, thought he was being virtuous. To express her joy she bought a tiny lamp and lit it in praise of such practice. In doing so, she gained the same amount of merit that the merchant would have acquired had his motivation been pure, while he accumulated great non-virtue.

Virtue and its opposite are not determined by the external form of an action but by the mental motivation. If you seek fame through hearing or practising a doctrine, you are not being virtuous. Therefore, before you start any practice or study, it is extremely important to turn your mind inward and adjust your motive. If your mind follows the Bodhisattva motivation, then your virtuous practice will be such that it cannot be lessened by poorer states of consciousness. When conjoined with an altruistic motivation, your practices will be like those of a being of greatest capacity. Such a being can generate the Bodhisattva motivation in connection with anything he does.

Two collections are necessary to attain Buddhahood: (i) that of conceivable merit, which is made by virtuous activities such as giving, ethics, patience, and so on; (ii) that of inconceivable wisdom, which is the virtue arising from meditation on emptiness. When a person has the Bodhisattva motivation and dedicates his actions to the welfare of all sentient beings, then no matter which of the two types he is collecting his acts will have limitless effects.

If you do not know how to engage in this motivation, then whether you listen to, think on, or meditate on the doctrine, your activity will be but an image of practice. Thus, it is essential to include the altruistic motivation of a Bodhisattva in whatever you do. Whether you are hearing, practising, meditating, reciting mantra, bowing down, circumambulating a reliquary, or reciting a single *om mani padme hūm*, you should join your activity with the Bodhisattva motivation – an aspiration induced by love and compassion for highest enlightenment for the sake of all sentient beings. It is called a mind of enlightenment, and it can transmute whatever you do into limitless meritorious power.

Avalokiteshvara is the quintessence of the compassion of all Buddhas, and his special mantra is *om mani padme hūm*. The white *om* symbolizes the body of all Buddhas. It cleanses the predispositions and defilements that would cause your rebirth as a god. Although the highest of the six types of cyclic existence, gods are unable to do the practices leading to liberation from cyclic existence, and thus birth as a god is to be avoided. Also, since *om* is the symbol of the body of all Buddhas, it clears away physical defilements and brings a brilliance to one's own body.

The demigods, the second highest type of cyclic existence, are especially afflicted with the suffering of jealousy. They see the wealth of the gods and are envious. As a result they make war with the gods in hopes of capturing that wealth. Through repeating the second syllable *ma* you can overcome the seeds and defilements of jealousy in yourself.

Through recitation of *ni* [which has a dot under it because the tongue is curled to the back of the mouth] you can cleanse the seeds and defilements that would cause you to be reborn as a human. Then the syllable *pad* will cleanse the seeds and predispositions that would cause you to be reborn as an animal – a being especially afflicted with stupidity.

By reciting *me* you can cleanse seeds and defilements that

would cause you to be reborn as a hungry ghost, whose special sufferings are hunger and thirst. Through the force of reciting *hūṃ* you overcome the seeds and defilements that would cause rebirth as a hell-being. In other words, the predispositions established by an act of hatred can be cleansed through this syllable.

By reciting Avalokiteshvara's mantra, you cause him, as if powerlessly, to shed whatever help he has on you and, by extension, on all sentient beings. The potential of his helpful power is vast. Ananda once asked Buddha why the earth had suddenly begun to tremble. Buddha answered that the great Bodhisattva Avalokiteshvara had arrived from a pure land and that due to the force of his tremendous power of manifestation and emanation the world itself was shaking. Ananda asked how Avalokiteshvara, a Bodhisattva, could possibly have such great power. Buddha explained that he only assumes the form of a high Bodhisattva but in fact is the emanator of most Buddhas.

If I went on to tell you all the benefits of reciting *oṃ maṇi padme hūṃ* or all the marvellous qualities of Avalokiteshvara we would never finish. Let us pass on to the motivation of a tantrist, a practitioner of the Secret Mantra Vehicle. The tantric motivation, built on the Bodhisattva aspiration to enlightenment for the sake of all sentient beings, has extensive skilful means.

There are two divisions within Mahayana: sutra and tantra. Tantra, or the Mantra Vehicle, has many skilful means to lead beings to highest enlightenment, and thus the process of enlightenment takes place much more quickly than in the sutra vehicle. Within Shakyamuni Buddha's teaching, the Mantra Vehicle is supreme. It is also called the Vajra Vehicle because a vajra symbolizes an immutable fusion of wisdom and compassion.

Secret Mantra is like a house in the middle of a broad field which can be entered from any direction: east, south, west or north. A student is not forced to a particular entrance, for there is a path to accommodate any trainee. In the lower vehicles one must follow a rather narrow path, but in the Mahayana Mantra Vehicle there are many extrardinary means of quickly amassing the collections of merit and wisdom. These collections are sources of power, and because tantra has ways of rapidly accumulating merit and wisdom, it is possible to achieve enlightenment quickly and rather easily. This ease and swiftness is a special feature of tantra.

In Buddhism there are nine different vehicles or systems of practice which will take you somewhere in the sense of increasing your understanding and profound realization. Only tantra, consisting of the last six vehicles, has these quick methods. If people put these methods into practice, they will each understand that the Secret Mantra Vehicle has many profound and quick ways of achieving enlightenment. Yet, no matter how profound the doctrine, no matter how swift the potential progress, if a trainee has no interest or aspiration, nothing will happen. Whether or not any good comes out of your practice depends on your will; tantras or any other doctrines are merely secondary conditions. Everything depends on your own aspiration, interest and will to achieve. If you have these primary inner conditions, then by relying on a spiritual guide you will be able to experience the profound quick path yourself.

The heart of all motivation lies in training your own thought. When you practise the motivation of Secret Mantra, you must change your attitude towards the place where the doctrine is being explained. For instance, forget that you are in a building constructed of solid material and consider it as a most marvellous mansion of light.

To Buddhists the best of all places is that where the Truth Body (*Dharmakāya*) resides. This is called the highest pure land. We are to train or cleanse our sense of the building's appearance and think that it is the highest pure land itself. Further, the teacher should not be considered a common being but a Truth Body. Students listening to the teaching should not see themselves and their companions as ordinary beings but as the retinue of the glorious Truth Body, consisting of the five Buddha lineages – in other words, as members of the transmission through the Conqueror's thought or of the transmission through the symbols of the Knowledge Bearers, or as male and female Bodhisattvas, or gods and goddesses.

The founder of the Nying-ma system is Padmasambhava, and thus the place of teaching could be thought of as the lotus-like palace on the glorious Copper-Coloured Mountain, the teacher as Padmasambhava himself, and the listeners as the eight Knowledge Bearers, very special people whose nature is light.

Or, you can conceive the place of teaching as the Eastern Pure Land called Great Delight. In that case the teacher would be Vajrasattva or Vajradhara. The latter means 'one who holds a vajra', indicating that he has an unchangeable mind – an immutable understanding of emptiness fused with compassion. Everyone in the room is part of the divine company of the vajra lineage, male and female Bodhisattvas – compassionate and knowing the very essence of the meaning of emptiness.

If you prefer, the place can be visualized as the Western Pure Land called the Joyous. The teacher can then be considered the Buddha Amitabha, and those listening to the doctrine the divine company of the lotus lineage, male and female Bodhisattvas, and gods and goddesses. These gods and goddesses are not part of cyclic existence, but very special beings who understand and are capable of practising all the various teachings.

Why should we visualize all this? It is a means of purifying the environment and the beings in it. Usually we think wrongly about the environment and beings, and this error draws us in to cyclic existence. Thus we need to train our minds in the substitution of appearances. Everything we see is to be viewed as Buddha Bodies. All sounds are to be heard as Buddha speech, continually explaining doctrine. All conceptions are to be viewed as emanations of the play of

Buddha wisdom. Finally, only endless purity will appear.

When a person has trained in these substitutions and is capable of using them in ordinary life, then at death when all usual appearances disappear, it is possible for him to manifest a whole pure land himself. For instance, we talk about the three unfortunate realms – hell-beings, hungry ghosts, and animals – as if they were far away, but in fact if we fall into hatred, greed, or stupidity, those three are here right now. The endless suffering that beings undergo is created by error about internal and external phenomena, for all the great qualities of Buddhas and Bodhisattvas arise from their ability to know their own mind. If you can come to know yours, you can manifest all these qualities, and you can transform yourself into a Buddha. If you do not know your own mind, you will keep falling back into cyclic existence, for just this knowledge is the dividing line between cyclic existence and nirvana. Whether you are listening to doctrine in a public place or studying in your own room, there is immense value in considering the place to have a special nature and in conceiving that the extraordinary Mahayana teaching is there in your hand. Such practices are a means of correcting the mind as well as the way we accept and conceive how these things appear. Whether or not these practices succeed depends on your mindfulness and introspection.

These substitutions are not false visualizations. It is not a matter of first thinking your surroundings are ordinary and then replacing them by something that is fantastic but false. You are to conceive them as having been this way from the very beginning and that you are identifying their own proper nature. Your senses normally misrepresent what is there, but through this visualization you can come closer to what actually exists.

The Three Jewels – Buddha, his Doctrine, and the Spiritual Community – are the three sources of refuge. A lama is the essence of these. His body is the spiritual community, his word is the excellent doctrine, and his mind is a Buddha.

The lama is considered to be the Three Buddha Bodies. His mind is the Truth Body, his speech is an Enjoyment Body, his body is an Emanation Body. The lama is an emanation of all past Buddhas, the source of the manifestation of all future Buddhas, and the embodiment of all present Buddhas.

The present aeon is called auspicious because a thousand Buddhas will appear in it. Due to our own contaminated actions and afflictions, we could not be trained by the former Buddhas. Therefore, the lama's kindness in training us is in a sense greater than that of all the Buddhas. In other words, because the Buddhas could not tame us while appearing in their own form, they now appear as teachers. A Buddha can manifest in many different forms, and even if your teacher cannot, he is said to be even greater than all Buddhas because their blessed empowerment and teachings flow through him to students. He serves as a waterway between his students and all Buddhas of the past, present and future. If this were cut, there would be no way for a student to reach the water. In this way, the teacher embodies the complete transmission from the، Buddhas themselves. Thus, the road or channel through which a student can receive the Buddhas' marvellous teaching is a teacher.

Of course, the teacher should not think, 'I am very important, I am infallible.' The teacher is only a bridge between Buddhas and students; so, he has no cause to be proud, he is only in the middle. If students and teacher think of it in this way, practice serves as a means to transmit the Buddhas' empowering blessings.

Students also are to be regarded as extraordinary beings, and here again this is not just imagination. They actually are out of the ordinary because their own basis is the Buddha nature, the Tathagata essence. Everyone has the nature and essence of a Buddha, and is capable of becoming a Buddha. From this point of view, all sentient beings are special. Their present life support is a precious human body, an amazing treasure, very difficult to achieve. Also, the secondary condition for attaining Buddhahood is present now in that they are all under the guidance of a spiritual teacher through whose precepts they will achieve higher states of mind. From these points of view they are all very special.

Whether a being is a tiny bug or a human endowed with the opportunities and conditions to achieve the doctrine, each has his own share of Buddha nature. At present it is obscured by the temporary defilements of desire, hatred and ignorance, but these are not part of a person's essential nature; they are accidental and can be removed.

When a person becomes capable of removing these temporary defilements, he will turn into a Buddha in and of himself. He does not have to acquire a Buddha nature because he has always had it.

3   Listening to Instructions

The activity of listening to instruction has two parts: abandoning hindrances and adopting aids.[8]

The first group of hindrances are the three faults of a receptacle. If your mind is distracted and does not pay attention to the lama's teaching, it is as if a receptacle or vessel were turned upside down and therefore unable to receive anything. That is the first fault.

The second is that even though the vessel may be upright, it leaks. No matter how much is poured in, nothing is retained. The third fault is to mix whatever you hear with afflictions of desire, hatred, or ignorance. For example, if there were poison in an otherwise suitable vessel and if you then added food or drink, that too would become poisonous.

How ought you to listen to doctrine? You should be like a deer listening to a guitar. It becomes so enthralled that a hunter can easily approach from behind or from the side and shoot it. Your ear-consciousness should be such that even if someone were coming to kill you, you would pay no attention. You would have no fear, for your mind would be completely fixed on what you were being taught.

Whenever you hear, think or meditate on the doctrine, you should not be distracted. For example, in northern Tibet there are nomads called Avaho who keep sheep. When they shear them, they take the wool in one hand while holding a knife in the other. Unless they are very careful, they will cut either their own hand or the sheep. They have to keep their mind one-pointedly on what they are doing. When you meditate, you should be like a dumb person tasting something. His mind is so concentrated that he pays attention only to the taste. You should be like this when you meditate.

Also, when you understand a doctrine, you should not become inflated by what you have done, but look to see what you should do next and get on with that. In Tibet there are large animals called yaks, and when they eat grass they do not watch the spot where their mouth is but the one that they will move to next. Be like them.

When experiencing the effect of these practices, you should be like the sun coming free of the clouds – without any sense of doubt but with brilliant clarity.

In short, when hearing the teaching, you should not allow your mind to flow to whatever thought arises but keep it on what is being taught. If thought is allowed to pass to external objects, then even though your body may be close to the doctrine, your mind will be totally unrelated with it, and it cannot help you at all. For example, there are people who, when they go to a lecture, chat with their friends about, perhaps, a war or some trouble they are planning for someone else. All such activities must be dropped. Even practices such as reciting mantra are to be set aside. Such recitation is in general a virtuous activity but out of place when listening to the teaching.

It is necessary to retain what is taught and to practise it continually. A Buddha can do nothing more for us than to explain the ways of achieving liberation. It must be understood that liberation depends on the student himself; whether you go on the path to omniscience or not depends upon you. The teaching should become so important that just reflecting on how pleasant it is to hear doctrine will cause the hairs of your body to stir and tears to well from your eyes. As a physical expression of this joy a student often joins his palms together near his heart in a gesture of respect.

SIX TAINTS OF HEARING

The second group of hindrances to be abandoned are the six taints of hearing. These are (i) pride, or thinking that you are superior to the lama who is explaining doctrine, (ii) having no faith in it, (iii) not diligently seeking it, (iv) being distracted by external objects, (v) withdrawing the senses inside too much, and (vi) fatigue.

Among the afflictions, pride and jealousy are particularly difficult to identify. To know them you must analyse your own mind in detail. For example, if you have a good mental quality, pride can cause you to generate such self-satisfaction that you are blind to your own defects. You become so inflated over your tiny virtue that you are unable to see another's good qualities, in which case you are unable to recognize a qualified teacher. Pride causes contempt of the lower, jealousy of the higher, and competitiveness with the equal. The water of spiritual attainments cannot collect on the iron lump of pride. Therefore, abandon pride, always identifying your own faults, exposing your defects, and assuming a humble posture.

NO FAITH

The very door of entry to the doctrine is faith. If you have none, the door of entry to practice is blocked.

Faith is of four types. The first is a mental clarity, a feeling of 'How wonderful!' when you see a lama or special religious place or attend a lecture. The second type of faith is the wish to attain whatever good qualities you see in others or read about in books. Once you have seen the marvellous qualities of a lama and been delighted by them, causing a wish to attain them, you will be able to understand them through practice. This is called the faith of conviction –

unshakable knowledge of virtuous qualities. When your knowledge of these becomes so clear that it is impossible to turn away from them, you have the fourth type of faith which is irreversible. Irreversible faith is based on knowledge arising from practice and cannot be lost; it merely grows stronger and stronger.

Diligent search for the doctrine is the very foundation of the auspicious qualities that are attained through practice. According to whether your diligence is great, middling, or small, so will be your practice and attainments. Even in worldly talk it is said that religion has no master – there is no one who will call one person higher and another lower. Through diligence you can become the highest, a Buddha.

Buddha himself met with a teacher who said that if he wanted to progress in doctrine, he must scrape out a thousand small cup-like holes in his body and insert wicks for candles. The teacher was actually a demon trying to lead Buddha on a wrong path, and later he told him that in order to receive another stanza of doctrine he would have to jump into a pit of fire. Finally he said that unless he would knock a thousand nails in his body, he could not receive another stanza of doctrine. Buddha did all this. He was misled by a false teacher, but he showed diligence, so that in the end he was able to purify his own consciousness and attain highest enlightenment.

In a sutra it is said, 'Seek the excellent doctrine until death, crossing through fire or on a razor's edge.' You should not worry about difficulties such as whether you will get hot or cold or have to listen for a long time. It will be to your great advantage to bear willingly whatever hardship is required.

DISTRACTION

What are the various objects by which the five senses can be distracted? The eye-consciousness can see forms – colours and shapes; the ear-consciousness can hear sounds; the nose-consciousness can smell odours; the tongue-

consciousness can experience tastes; the body-conscious-
ness can experience tangible objects.

Attachment to the objects of the five senses and of the
mental consciousness is the root of all our suffering. All the
various sufferings in cyclic existence arise from attachment
to these six types of things. For instance, through the
attachment of its eye-consciousness to colour and shape, a
moth flies into a flame and kills itself. To a moth, the light is
so attractive that it cannot keep away from it but has to go to
it. The fire is so alluring that he keeps returning to it in spite
of the pain. Also a deer, as was mentioned earlier, is so
attracted by the sound of a guitar that a hunter can easily
approach and kill it. A bee, through being attached to the
scent of a flower, will sometimes be caught inside one. A
fish is overly attached to taste, and when a fisherman lowers
a baited hook, the fish rushes for it. An elephant is attracted
by the feeling of mud and sinks into it, unable to escape.

The source or mother of all of these distractions is the
mental consciousness, for it allows the sense-
consciousnesses to go out and be caught. Also, if when
hearing, thinking, or meditating on the doctrine, your mind
wanders to a past event, you will quickly become so lost in
that thought that you have no hope of retaining the object of
your concentration.

You will be equally distracted if your mind runs to the
future and begins to muse about possible events. Also, if
you become distracted by what is taking place around you,
you can neither hear, think, nor meditate; therefore, you
should set your mind one-pointedly on its object.

Whether you are attending to an object of meditation, of
thinking, or of hearing, do not think about what you did in
the past, for it has already disappeared like writing on
water.

If when hearing or meditating you are distracted by
anything, remember that this, like all things, is impermanent. Let your thought dwell awhile on how wealth is
gathered and again dispersed, how trouble arises and then

subsides. Merely by understanding their impermanence, your mind will cease to flow to them. Then you can return to your meditation.

You may feel, I won't practise now, I will make money first. However, it is foolish to think on what the future may bring and better to reduce wishes and desires. For you cannot tell when you will die, but it will probably be before you have had a chance to effect all these plans.

Therefore, to indulge in planning is like fishing in a dry ravine filled with rocks, hoping that water will cover them. If something does come to mind about the future, think about the uncertainty of the time of death. It is definite that we will die, but the time is indefinite. Once you see that death is definite, but not when it will occur, and that everything is impermanent, is there time for anything except practice?

Our present activities are like housekeeping in a dream. If you spend your dream-time keeping accounts and worrying about where to put your money, will it help you? Because our daily activities are mainly involved in mistaken appearances, they should be forsaken. You should not even be attached to food but use it simply to help your practices, taking just enough and not too much. Food may be pleasant for a very short time, but once you have swallowed it, the taste and smell will mean nothing to you. As is said:

Past deeds are like pictures in water, but afterwards
They do not exist, so do not dwell on them later.
If you remember something, think of the gathering
And dispersing of wealth and trouble. What else can
You do but practise, O reciters of mantra?

To plan for the future is like fishing a dry ravine,
So fall not into thought, but reduce wishes and desires.
If you remember something, think how unsure is the time of
   death.
How can there be time for aught but practice, O reciters of
   mantra?

All that you do now is like housekeeping
In a dream, so cease such senseless toil.
Take with the seal of non-attachment food helpful to your
     practice,
For your actions have no essence, O reciters of mantra.

This practice, taming the conceptions of the three poisons –
Desire, hatred, and delusion – after meditation,
Is needed 'til all things shine as the Truth Body
Remember it when needed, be not distracted
By mistaken thoughts, O reciters of mantra.

The forms and thoughts now arising in our minds have a strong element of mistake; be careful that they do not distract you.

If your mind is full of useless thoughts of the future and welcomes them as harbingers, you will be like Moon-Fame's father. In the past a poor man came upon a heap of barley which he put in a bag and hung up in the rafters above his bed to keep it safe from mice and robbers. He lay down and thought, 'Now I can make barley beer and sell it for money; then I can take a nice young wife, and she will certainly give birth to a boy.' He lay there wondering, 'What shall I name the boy?' He glanced through his window and saw that the moon was rising. Thinking that his child would be as widely known and famous as the moon, he decided, 'I shall call him Moon-Fame.' Meanwhile, a mouse on the rafter was eating the rope holding the barley. When the rope broke, the bag fell on his head and killed him. This story is so well-known in Tibet that we frequently warn someone by saying, 'You are becoming like Moon-Fame's father!'

You will never have time to carry out all the thoughts and desires that come to your mind, so do not let yourself be distracted by them. Listen to the teaching with mindfulness and attentiveness.

Even if you are not distracted by thoughts of the past or future, you can be hindered by a grasping attentiveness, concentrating so much on each phrase that continuity is lost; with each new topic the previous one is forgotten. A bear who wants to catch mice living in a hole scratches at the ground until they start to run out. He snatches up the first one that appears and tucks it up his backside. Having done this, he immediately bends down to catch a second mouse, and the moment he leans over, the first one jumps out. He takes the second mouse, tucks it away, and as he reaches for the third mouse, the second one jumps out. This can happen with doctrine too. When your attention passes too strongly from one topic to another, you may lose your grasp of the continuity.

WITHDRAWAL

If your mind is too withdrawn, it is also impossible to listen well. The teacher's words come from without, but if your mind is withdrawn deep inside, it will not meet with the teaching, and you will easily fall into sleep and obscuration. Therefore, you must moderate the tightness and looseness of your mind.

A monk named Shrona was trying to learn meditation, but his mind was either too tight or too lose. So he went to Buddha for advice and said, 'I cannot meditate at all, what shall I do?'

Buddha asked, 'When you were a householder, surely you played the violin well?'

Shrona answered, 'Yes, indeed.'

Buddha asked, 'Was the sound right when you tightened the strings very strongly, or when you loosened them very thoroughly?'

'Neither. I had to do it with moderation.'

'In the same way,' Buddha told him, 'you have to moderate the tightness and looseness of your mind in order to meditate.'

Shrona took his advice, and his meditation developed well. He was able to vanquish desire, hatred and ignorance, thereby attaining the rank of an Arhat.

Similar advice was given by a famous female adept in Tibet, Ma-ji-lap-drön (*Ma-cig-lab-sgron*):

First tighten with tightness,
Then loosen with looseness.
The view's essence is here.

If you do not first tighten your mind strongly, it will spread out among many different thoughts. Then, when your mind is concentrated enough not to be caught in a rush of thoughts, loosen it slightly within the state of tightness. This teaching contains a very important essential of the view because this is the moment when you can begin to understand.

DISCOURAGEMENT

Discouragement may arise, for example, at the prospect of a long lecture on doctrine. In Tibet, lectures often lasted four or five hours and still do in the refugee communities in India. Before going you may feel that your back or thighs will ache badly. That is the moment to generate patience and delight in hearing, so that these discomforts can simply be forgotten.

If you think that a practice or session will be difficult, you can clear your mind by appraising your own situation. Recall that you now have a body of opportunities and conditions and that it is very difficult to be born with a chance to practise. Remember also that you have met with the teaching of a qualified lama and take joy in his profound precepts. Realize that the opportunity to hear such discourse is very rare and that to be able to hear this excellent doctrine now is due to your having amassed a great deal of merit over many lifetimes.

The present is indeed an amazing opportunity, because the help from study and practice will last through many lives. It is as if you are being offered a single meal that will nourish and sustain you all your life. Therefore, be willing to accept with patience whatever difficulties may arise.

FIVE NON-RETENTIONS

    (i) Retaining the words but not the meaning
   (ii) Retaining the meaning but not the words
  (iii) Retaining the meaning without identifying it
  (iv) Retaining the meaning but confusing the order
   (v) Retaining the wrong meaning.

Retaining the words but not the meaning is when you remember the words if they are beautiful or appealing but pay no attention to what they mean. Retaining the meaning but not the words occurs, for instance, if after hearing a discourse on impermanence, you have a vague recollection that impermanence was taught but cannot recall how, or the different aspects of the doctrine.

Not identifying the meaning is to make a vague assumption about a word or phrase without accurate knowledge or to accept literally teachings that require interpretation. To confuse the order is, for example, to remember Hinayana precepts as Mahayana ones.

With regard to retaining the wrong meaning, whether you are listening to instructions on view, meditation, or practice, if you retain the wrong meaning, your practice will be inverted. For instance, when you hear the Mahayana teaching, you may take in the words easily, but unless you understand them properly you can fall to the extremes of permanence and annihilation.

FOUR RIGHT DISCRIMINATIONS

Four thoughts, about yourself, the teaching, the teacher and your practice, are the four right discriminations. Think of yourself as sick and the doctrine as your medicine; consider the lama to be a highly skilled doctor and earnest practice as taking the medicine.

Put aside the conventional thought of yourself as healthy. We are all sick in that since beginningless time we have been polluted by the three afflictions of desire, hatred and

ignorance. This sickness is so pervasive that we do not call it
an illness. For example, when someone becomes delirious
with a high temperature, he does not know that he has a
fever. He accepts all his perceptions as valid and acts
accordingly. In the same way we are crazed by the afflictions
of desire, hatred and ignorance. An illness in this life can at
the most cause our death, but this beginningless illness of
desire, hatred and ignorance has caused us to die and be
reborn in life after life.

Conventional medicine will not help this illness; yet,
unless some is taken, the disease will never be cured. The
medicine that will help is a mixture of excellent doctrine and
religious practice. In order to learn how to take it, you must
rely on a spiritual guide. A conventional doctor can help the
various disorders that affect the physical body, but only a
spiritual guide can dispense the medicine that will cure the
afflictions that we have had since beginningless time. This
guide is the ultimate doctor of the mind.

Buddha spoke many sutras and tantras, and his followers
have written many commentaries that set forth the essen-
tials of medicinal doctrine. A spiritual guide gathers these
different medicines from the teachings of Buddha and gives
them to his students in accordance with their illness. A
spiritual guide has not just read Buddha's teaching but has
experienced its meaning and knows the diseases of mind
that particular teachings will help. He regards a student as
his own child and prescribes for it because there is no one
else able to do so. With great love and warmth he gives
special medicine to his children. This is called the extraordinary thought of a spiritual guide. But if students do not
take the medicine, it will do no good; its usefulness depends
entirely on the student. Buddha himself said 'I am giving
you the means of liberation. Know that its attainment
depends on you.'

Death may come at any time, so start to practise
immediately. You might wonder, 'Even if I did die, would I
not have a chance to attain Buddhahood in the future?'

When you die, you pass into bardo – an intermediate state between this and the next life. At that time your mind is like a bird blown about in a gale, or a dog left by its master in the middle of a city, running here and there. Great happiness and suffering are both possible in this state, but it is too late to think about practising the path.

Because the mind encounters such difficulties in the intermediate state, it is impossible to change course and to head away from a bad to a happy migration as you would direct a horse by pulling the right or left rein; not even a priest can help you now. Because of your former actions you are blown to the edge of a high cliff over a huge chasm into which you will fall if you err in the slightest.

Like a snake in a section of bamboo, you can go only one way or the other. Although the pressure towards an unfortunate realm is very severe, you have to tread a narrow path to a happy rebirth. Now is the time to practise, to transform your mind by maturing the four right discriminations and by always avoiding the four wrong ones.

FOUR WRONG DISCRIMINATIONS

The first is to compare a lama to a musk deer instead of a doctor. The second is to think of the doctrine as musk instead of medicine. The third is to treat practice as a way to kill your lama (the musk deer), instead of a means of taking medicine. The fourth is to regard yourself as a hunter instead of a sick person.

How does one come to have such ideas? There are deer in Tibet and elsewhere which secrete the best musk. In the same way, a student who thought his lama had valuable doctrine might feel, 'If I can replace him, I will be famous.' Instead of practising doctrine, he strives to overcome his teacher, and to use the doctrine for his own purposes. Thus, he is like a hunter who seeks musk deer because he knows its fragrant scent will bring money. The student is seeking prestige, respect and even wealth.

Whenever you find tendencies towards this wrong discrimination in yourself, strive to discard them. If you have a mistaken idea of your relationship with a teacher and his teaching, improper reliance on him will serve as a means for accumulating great non-virtue. Actions based on such mistaken discrimination will only bring you suffering; discard it and always make right discriminations.

SIX PERFECTIONS

The six perfections are applied at all levels of training in the path, but here specifically to the practice of listening to instruction. They are giving, ethics, patience, effort, concentration and wisdom.

Before you hear doctrine, give by scattering flowers and rice round the lama's seat. Cleaning the place where the doctrine is taught is an act of ethics. Refraining from anger during the lecture when disturbed by others is an instance of practising patience. Striving to generate the faith of conviction in the teacher and the teachings is practice of the perfection of effort. Setting your mind one-pointedly on the teaching and not letting it wander to external objects is to practise the perfection of concentration. Questioning the teacher about doubts that have arisen is to practise the perfection of wisdom.

In this way you can practise all six perfections within the activity of listening to doctrine. The same applies to a lama in his teaching. His explanation of doctrine without hope for goods, praise, or fame is an act of giving; his not despising other teachers is an instance of ethics; not angering when others repeat questions is patience; not becoming discouraged though teaching night and day is effort; directing the mind to the words and meaning is concentration; and realizing the non-inherent existence of teacher, teaching and the taught as well as generating in students the wisdom of hearing and thinking, is the practice of wisdom.

4 Opportunities and Conditions

Opportunity means freedom from the eight conditions of non-leisure so that you have the time and opportunity to practise the doctrine.[9] The eight conditions of non-leisure are:

(i)   birth as a hell-being
(ii)   birth as a hungry ghost
(iii)   birth as an animal
(iv)   birth as a god of long life
(v)   birth in an uncultured area
(vi)   birth as a person having wrong views
(vii)   birth in a land where a Buddha has not been
(viii)   birth as a stupid person.

The hells are places of rebirth, and even though they are impermanent, while you are there, you suffer night and day from extreme heat or cold. Thus it is difficult to practise doctrine in the hells.

If you are born as a hungry ghost, you are so afflicted by the sufferings of hunger and thirst that you also have no chance to practise doctrine.

If you are born among the animals that are scattered about the surface of the earth, you will probably suffer by being made use of by others. Penned up and finally killed, your flesh will be sold for food. If you are born in the sea, you will face the problem of the larger eating the smaller and the smaller living off the larger.

If you are born as a god of long life, you are in a state like deep sleep such that you cannot even think about practising doctrine.

If you are born as a barbarian, that is to say, in an uncultured area where Buddha's teaching has not spread, then no matter how able you are, you cannot hear doctrine.

If you are born in a country or family whose thought is dominated by views opposed to Buddhist teaching and if you accept them, you are prevented from practising doctrine.

If you are born in a land where a Buddha has not been or where his teaching has not appeared, you cannot even hear the word 'Buddha' or 'Buddhist doctrine'.

If you are born stupid, then your consciousness is not adequate to listen to or practise the doctrine.

These are called the eight conditions of non-leisure because if you are born into any one of them you have no opportunity to hear or practise the path of liberation. Those born in the three lower realms – hell-beings, hungry ghosts, and animals – have to undergo extreme suffering. Animals are especially afflicted by stupidity, hungry ghosts by hunger and thirst, hell-beings by hot and cold. Their lives are so completely dominated by these sufferings that practice is almost impossible.

A barbarous or uncultured area is where, for instance, people kill their enemies with poisoned arrows. Barbarian religions teach one to kill sentient beings, slit their throats, and offer their blood and flesh to spirits. Even if Buddha himself came to such people and explained the advantages of practising Buddhism, they would not listen to him or change their habits. Even if they had not been misled by a false doctrine, their present skill in killing all and sundry for sacrifice would condemn them to be reborn in an extremely unfortunate realm.

We tend to think that a god with a long life span leads a very comfortable and blissful existence. Yet this type of birth is also considered a condition of non-leisure mainly because gods are so immersed, for instance, in the meditation of infinite space or consciousness that they cannot imagine doing anything else. Since they mistakenly believe that this is the only path to Buddhahood, they feel no need to adopt any other type of practice. Since they do not develop a wisdom consciousness, we call this a state of distraction. Near the time of death they realize clairvoyantly the condition into which they are about to be reborn. Then, when they see their meditation by itself has not led them to Buddhahood, they decide that there is no such path.

People with wrong views hold beliefs that do not accord with the Buddhist views of impermanence, selflessness and so forth. This includes followers of contradictory religious or philosophical systems, as well as those who simply hate religion. Buddha himself had a servant who stayed with him for a long time but never showed any interest in doctrine. He did not have the seed of liberation from cyclic existence and remained stuck in his wrong ideas even though he was serving Buddha himself and could always listen to his teaching.

An aeon during which a Buddha does not appear is called dark. If you are born at such a time and even if you have sense enough to want to practise doctrine, you could not hear even the names of the Three Jewels – Buddha, Doctrine, and Spiritual Community.

Stupidity has two types, those of speech and of mind. One who is stupid in terms of speech can hear but cannot speak. Mental stupidity is a case where the person can hear but not understand what is said. Even when the doctrine is explained, he cannot comprehend it or practise a path to liberation.

If in looking at yourself you find that you have any of these eight factors, you are a person who has no opportunities.

To have conditions involves the five outer and five inner conditions. The five inner conditions are:

   (i)   birth as a human
  (ii)   birth in a central country where Buddha's teaching
         has spread
 (iii)   possession of all five senses
 (iv)   no commission of a heinous act
  (v)   faith in Buddha's teaching.

The five outer conditions are so called because they depend on the environment into which one is born:

   (i)   visitation of a Buddha to the area
  (ii)   his spoken doctrine
 (iii)   the doctrine remaining to the present
 (iv)   introduction to the teaching
  (v)   assistance from a spiritual guide.

Our world is a place which a Buddha visited. If after attaining Buddhahood he had remained in meditative stabilization without saying anything, it would be impossible for us to understand and practise his teaching. Also, if he had taught the doctrine but it had been lost, no one could hear about or practise it. Any thought of so doing would be useless if there were not someone in the area compassionate enough to practise and understand the doctrine, and to teach it to others. Without the aid of a spiritual guide the depths of the doctrine cannot be known.

    Ba-drul Rin-bo-chay follows a system that also details eight sudden impediments – sudden in that they can appear quickly at any time, causing one's opportunities and conditions to degenerate:

   (i)   influence from an evil force
  (ii)   disturbance by the five poisons
 (iii)   interruption
 (iv)   distraction by laziness
  (v)   servitude
 (vi)   seeking religion as protection from fear
(vii)   hypocrisy
(viii)   obscuration.

(i) Influence from an evil force. The influence of an evil teacher makes it impossible to practise correct doctrine. In India there was a monk who later became one of Buddha's most famous students. An evil teacher told him to kill a great number of people and collect their fingers. By the time he met Buddha, he had collected the fingers of 999 people. He was called Finger Garland (*Aṅgulimāla*) because he wore a garland of them round his neck. The antidote to such evil influence is to examine a spiritual guide and determine whether he has love and compassion.

(ii) Disturbance by the five poisons. The five poisons are desire, hatred, delusion, pride and competitiveness. These can arise with such force during meditation that it is impossible to continue. The antidote to desire is to reflect on ugliness; to hatred is to generate love; to delusion is to learn the differences between phenomena. The antidote to pride is to reflect on one's own constituents, and to competitiveness is to cultivate joy in others' success.

(iii) Interruption. We are often interrupted by internal or external circumstances. For instance, practice is impossible if as a result of our own past non-virtuous actions we become so sick that we require intense medical care. Through past non-virtuous actions we have created a force in the mind, much as drops of water become a great lake. This force remains dormant until something happens to release the water and we are drowned by this interruption. Sometimes we then lose faith in the cause and effect of actions because we think our auspicious practice should prevent such interruptions. Actually, the interruptions should lead us to discover greater depths in the cause and effect of actions. The antidote is to develop great belief in the inevitability of the effects of actions and be contrite for all the wrong we have done.

(iv) Distraction by laziness. To be distracted by laziness means to put off what you can do now. Buddhist doctrine may be difficult, but you can practise a little now. If you delay, you will finally die with deep regret for your procrastination. The antidote is to reflect on death and impermanence and to work hard.

(v) Servitude. If you are the slave of a great person, you have to wait on him continually so that even if you wish to practise doctrine, you have no time for it. The antidote is to search out a clever way to get free.

(vi) Seeking religion as protection from fear. This is very easily acquired. For instance, if someone becomes very sick, he suddenly – perhaps for the first time – turns his mind to spiritual practice. He is seeking to rid himself of a temporary ailment and not the ultimate sickness that keeps him in cyclic existence. The antidote is always to practise with a strong . wish to leave all cyclic existence and with an altruistic aspiration to Buddhahood. Religious motivation is not a mere search for protection from temporary fear; you should perceive cyclic existence in all its forms – pleasurable and painful – as a great whirlwind of fire and wish to remove yourself and all sentient beings from it.

(vii) Hypocrisy. Hypocrisy is to pretend to practise for the sake of receiving goods, services and respect. The antidote is to know the faults of thoughts and actions aimed at achieving welfare in this transient life and to abandon such intentions.

(viii) Obscuration. Having an obscured mind does not mean to be stupid but refers to the extreme obscuration of someone who aspires to leave cyclic existence, and does not practise for the sake of liberating all sentient beings and establishing them in Buddhahood. Although superior to one who has no wish to leave cyclic existence, he is said to be obscured because his mind cannot accommodate the larger motivation that would include others who suffer in the same way as he. The antidote is to confess former misdeeds and petition the god of wisdom, Manjushri.

A person with any of these eight conditions of non-leisure

can have only a form or image of religious practice. Though it is difficult to be free from all these, Ba-drul Rin-bo-chay includes another final list of eight non-leisures that are called deprivations because they deprive us of the paths of liberation and omniscience:

   (i)   little discouragement for cyclic existence
  (ii)   no wealth of faith
 (iii)   being bound by the chains of desire and attachment
 (iv)   coarse behaviour
  (v)   no shame at non-virtue
 (vi)   mistaken modes of behaviour
(vii)   breaking a vow
(viii)   breaking pledges.

To have little discouragement or renunciation means that you are so attached to cyclic existence that your disillusionment with the round of birth, ageing, sickness and death is very slight. In order to practise Buddhism correctly, it is necessary to have a strong sense that cyclic existence is an endless round of pain. You should feel that it is like living on the point of a needle, that there is no pleasure in it. You are stimulated into thinking that the only sensible activity is practice.

The best of all wealth is faith – a sense of clear delight in the path and its fruits. Unless you are motivated by this delight, you cannot succeed in cultivating the path.

Some people have so much desire and attachment that if there is only a single piece of paper or a pencil left, they feel, 'I must have it, not you.' Their desire and attachment are so great that they cannot take into account other people's feelings. They are prevented from practice by their own desire and attachment.

Coarse behaviour is, for instance, fighting and quarrelling among students. If you want to practise, you should be soft and smooth, seeking to end quarrels.

Not being ashamed of your own lack of virtue means to engage in actions that you have identified as not virtuous

without any sense of shame. It is said that even if a
non-virtue is very small, you should not think that its effect
must be the same. If possible, do not engage in any
non-virtue, no matter how small it is, for just as a tiny spark
can set fire to a haystack, a tiny non-virtue can cause great
suffering. Tiny virtues can also have tremendous effects. A
mass of them will in time have great power, like the
accumulation – drop by drop – of water in a vessel.

A mistaken mode of behaviour here means to turn away
from Mahayana to Hinayana practices. Mahayana is capable
of bearing and fructifying the aims of all sentient beings
everywhere; therefore, if you reject it in preference to the
smaller attitude and motivation of Hinayana, it is a great
mistake.

Breaking vows refers, for instance, to the 253 vows of a
monk, the four pillars of which are not to kill, steal, speak
falsely about spiritual attainments, or copulate. If a monk
does so, he has broken his vow.

When a tantric lama initiates a student, the latter takes
pledges, many of which are concerned with the relationship
between himself and the lama. If the student does not keep
his pledges, he involves himself in the last of the eight
conditions of deprivation: breaking pledges.

Thus, there are thirty-four prerequisites for a full and
correct practitioner: eight opportunities, ten conditions,
and sixteen additional opportunities. Possession of them is
a limitless treasure. All of us have done actions that are
capable of impelling us into any of the conditions of
non-leisure. Therefore, before harmful conditions suddenly
arise, it is suitable to petition Padmasambhava for help so
that you may not come under the influence of these
obscurations and interruptions.

DIFFICULTY OF OBTAINING
OPPORTUNITIES AND CONDITIONS

Our system of a thousand million worlds can be thought of
as an ocean. Imagine that an ox-yoke is floating on the

ocean, at the mercy of winds and currents. A blind turtle lives under the water and every hundred years comes up for air. How often would it happen to surface through the yoke? That is how often we obtain a life of opportunities and conditions like the one we now have.

The ocean symbolizes the unlimited sufferings of the three lower realms. The blindness of the turtle refers to the ignorance of what to adopt and discard. Surfacing every hundred years indicates the difficulty of freeing oneself. The hole in the yoke suggests the limited number of humans and gods. The movement of the yoke in the wind refers to the fact that birth in a fortunate realm is influenced by virtues.

This analogy was given by Buddha himself. Nagarjuna, a great Mahayana master, quoted it in his *Friendly Letter* (*Suhrllekha*) to the Indian king Shatavahana as did Shantideva in his *Engaging in the Bodhisattva Deeds* (*Bodhisattvacharyāvatāra*), saying that it is even harder to attain opportunities and conditions than for a turtle to surface through the yoke.

Another way to understand the difficulty of attaining a human life is to think of handfuls of dried peas thrown against a pane of glass. The chances of attaining a human life are less than those of a pea sticking to the glass. Or, if you drop handfuls of mustard seed on the point of a needle, how many seeds would be pierced? There are even fewer instances of attaining a human body.

If the number of hell-beings equals the number of stars visible on a clear night, the number of hungry ghosts is the same as that of stars seen during the day. Again, if the number of hungry ghosts is illustrated by that of stars at night, the number of animals is equal to that of stars during the day. If the number of animals is that of stars on a clear night, then the number of beings in the fortunate realms is like that of stars seen during the day. If you count all the humans who have no religious practice and engage in many non-virtues, those who practise what Buddha taught are again like stars in daytime. Relatively speaking, birth in a fortunate realm endowed with opportunities and conditions is extremely rare.

When we debate on relativity, we say that a 4-inch line is long in relation to a 1-inch line, but short compared with an 8-inch one. This illustrates the reasoning by which all conventional phenomena are shown to be relative. They exist in dependence on something else. Therefore, it would be a lie to say that anything exists in and of itself.

Take another example. The number of hell-beings is equal to the number of grains of sand in the whole world. There are as many hungry ghosts as grains of sand along the Ganges River, and as many animals as the grains in a handful of sand. The number of gods and humans, which are beings born in the fortunate realms, equals that of the grains on the tip of a fingernail. Also, within the fortunate realms, it is extremely rare to have a life-support of opportunities and conditions.

If it seems to you that there are a great many human beings, think how many more other types of beings there are. How many sentient beings would you find in one ant hill in comparison with the number of human beings who would fill your room? Among human beings themselves, consider how many have the eight opportunities or the ten conditions.

Among all peoples in the world, it would be very difficult to find many who are supported by opportunities and conditions. So many human beings are involved in war or the supply of weapons. They are far better off than many other sentient beings, but they have no opportunities or conditions. Thus, they are said to have a secondary human life-support. Although they have achieved a human body, they are unable to perform the essential practices. It is the ability to practise that makes human life valuable.

There are said to be jewels that grant anything you wish, but this life of opportunities and conditions is far more valuable than any such gem. It is far more profitable to take the Bodhisattva vows than to have the resources of a king:

these can be exhausted and are worth nothing compared to the continuous help that arises from vows.

The great Tibetan yogi Mi-la-re-ba once told a hunter that a life of opportunities and conditions is very rare, but for a person like him it was non-existent.

Shantideva said that someone who has opportunities and conditions and does not take joy in it is extremely foolish. If, after analysing, you find that you have the ten conditions and the eight opportunities, you should not despise yourself by thinking you are poor.

For example, we have the opportunities that free us from the first set of impediments. We have been born as humans with all our faculties and in a land to which Buddha's teaching has spread. We have not committed any horrors that would prevent our religious practice, and we have faith in Buddha and his followers. Buddha came to this world and gave the teaching which lives on today. We ourselves are beginning to study it with the aid of spiritual guides.

In your meditation session, analyse point by point whether or not you have the qualities of opportunity. If you decide that you have them, concentrate on how rare they are. Practise stabilizing meditation with this as your object. If while doing so you begin to lose your sense of the rareness of opportunity, pass on to analytical meditation on conditions. Examine the ten qualities and determine how rare it is to attain them; then pass to stabilizing meditation, this time taking the rareness of conditions as your object. When your sense of this begins to weaken, turn to analytical meditation on the difficulty of finding opportunities and conditions.

Then, analyse in the same way the different types of living beings by considering the number of organisms in your own body – scripture says that there are 84,000 of them. Each of these organisms has a mind, so that for every human mind there are at least 84,000 animal ones. When you have understood the significance of this, remain in stabilizing meditation with your understanding.

Seeing that we have such a precious lifetime, we must be careful to avoid the influence of unfavourable circumstances. We are not troubled by sickness and suffering, we are not slaves but are free to do as we wish. These factors are dependent-arisings that coincide at the present. It is very helpful to engage in religious practice, but there are many interruptions. We do not know when we will die, but when death comes we will lose this precious life-support of opportunities and conditions. Our own body, which we hold so precious, will be taken from our bed and cremated or buried while our consciousness wanders among the lands of the intermediate state and we are forced to proceed alone to our next rebirth. If we have not practised and developed our minds, passing on to the next life can be a frightful experience. Therefore, we often request Guru Padmasambhava's aid so that in the time remaining before death we may be able to engage in valuable religious practice.

You should recognize that if you do not now make use of this precious base of opportunities and conditions, later you will not be able to find such a marvellous opportunity for achieving liberation. During this life you will merely consume your meritorious power and then be reborn in a lower realm where it will be impossible to hear doctrine or to meet with spiritual guides. The time to meditate is now.

How much should you meditate? A famous Ga–dam–ba (*bKa'-gdams-pa*) Ge-shay recited a mantra of one of the fierce deities nine hundred million times. He kept track of the number with his rosary. His teacher remarked, 'You will become worn out by so much recitation. Take it easy and have a little rest.' The Ge-shay answered, 'Yes, but when I think about this life of opportunities and conditions, I know there is no time to sleep.'

5 *Meditation on Impermanence*

Meditation on impermanence begins with reflection on the impermanence of the external world.[10] Formation of a world system, complete with sentient beings, takes twenty intermediate aeons; that of our environment takes nineteen aeons and of all the beings dwelling within a world system, one intermediate aeon.

The environment and its beings remain for a period of twenty intermediate aeons, which is followed by an equal period during which the world system is destroyed, after which there are twenty intermediate aeons of voidness. These eighty intermediate aeons make one great aeon.

At the onset of the first intermediate aeon of formation, the winds of the four directions blow against their opposite winds, thereby forming the shape of crossed vajras which support everything that is to follow. Great rains fall, and a circle of water forms on the vajras. Through churning, a layer of gold forms on the water, with another of stone and earth on top of it. On the layer of earth grow the forests and fields that we see.

Once the world system is formed, it lasts for twenty intermediate aeons, when it is destroyed by fire and flood. First a sun appears in the sky that is much brighter and hotter than our present one. In each of the next six days a new sun appears, burning everything from forests and mountains to oceans. After that, a great rain falls – so extraordinary that the earth finally dissolves in the water. Then the crossed vajras rise up with the result that nothing can be supported any longer, and the twenty aeons of voidness begin.

How can you apply this to meditation? Look at the world and think, 'If this great world is going to be destroyed and turned into a void, then of course my house will disintegrate. I should not be attached to these things which are inevitably going to fall apart.'

The next step is to meditate on impermanence by thinking about the migrating beings who dwell in the environment. For instance, recall famous people who appeared in the past, consider that not one of them is here now, they have all gone. They are finished.

You can then meditate on impermanence by thinking about holy persons such as Buddha and his famous disciples, Shariputra and Modgalyayana. All that is left of them now are stories. There were the eighty adepts and the six whose teaching was so great that they are considered adornments of the doctrine. All we have of them now are impoverished biographies.

Many incarnations of Avalokiteshvara appeared in Tibet in the form of religious kings, translators, scholars and adepts. What is left of them nowadays? Of that famous adept Padmasambhava only his biography survives. Contemporary with the Bodhisattva Shantarakshita were two hundred Indian and Tibetan translators who met together to render the scriptures from Sanskrit into Tibetan; not one of these remains today. The great yogi Mi-la-re-ba who could not be burned when he was thrust into a fire or drowned when he was thrown into water is not here either.

You can think about your own teachers; some of them may be dead by now. Reflect that if these very special people have died, you yourself will certainly do so.

Next you can meditate on impermanence by thinking about the lords of beings. Where are all the great kings of the past? You cannot meet with them. Like all the others they have followed their nature of impermanence.

Then meditate on the various examples and their meanings. Consider the change of the seasons. Think how trees, flowers and fields look in the summer and how quickly they change in the autumn and winter. This can give you a clear idea of the nature of impermanence. Everything that is made, everything that depends on causes, is affected by impermanence. If you look at a youthful photograph of an old friend, you feel immediately how good-looking he was, but now his flesh is wrinkling, there are old age spots on his face and he is beginning to look ugly.

You can then meditate on impermanence by thinking on the uncertainty of the causes of death. There are so many of them that we cannot be sure which will be the one. We cannot even be confident that we will not die tonight or tomorrow; many people die while walking from one place to another.

Sometimes people think, 'I am young, I do not need to worry about death.' But actually there is no certainty whether you will be young or old when you die. The thought, 'I will not die too soon,' is a matter of our not having used correct reasoning through being attached to our life. Nagarjuna said that, given the number of possible causes of death, not to die between two breaths was as amazing as that, after going to bed at night, we get up again in the morning.[11]

Since we are certain to die but uncertain when it will be, it is necessary to know what will help at death and afterwards. None of our possessions, authority, or power will assist. Only religious practice is of use because it furthers the mind which continues from one life to another. To practise well you must meditate on impermanence with a great sense of urgency by identifying it and probing into its meaning. Sometimes test your realization by going to a place where you usually feel happy, at others where you are frightened or sad.

The Ga-dam-ba Ge-shays were often so imbued with a sense of impermanence that they would not clean the offering bowls at night or wash and set out their own dishes for the next morning.

In your meditation you should consider your body as a place where you can rest for a little while. Since you will leave it, you should not be too attached to it, nor to the place where you live, which you should consider a pure land.

Food, drink and clothing are all impermanent and will disappear. Use them merely to take care of your life, and let them disappear of their own accord. No matter how nice or nasty some food or drink is, it only lasts between your tongue and your throat. Sleep itself is impermanent; you awaken and it ends. So try to make it useful by meditating on the clear light of dream.

If you prosper and attain great wealth, you should turn it into the seven wealths of a Superior – faith, ethics, giving, hearing, embarrassment, shame and wisdom. Worldly wealth is impermanent and disappears moment by moment, while that of a Superior helps life after life.

Everyone is impermanent; friends, enemies, and those who are neutral will all pass away. Cultivate the knowledge that neither they nor the environment are permanent. In this way you can develop a sense of discouragement for cyclic existence in general. Whether you are famous or powerful makes no difference. Your life is completely subject to uncertain causes and conditions; therefore, no matter what your worldly status may be, make yourself humble.

Even the faith that delights in the doctrine is impermanent. You may tend to listen to doctrine now because you have a little faith, but you should understand that your faith is impermanent and that the time to practise is now when you have it. Practice will enable you to abandon non-virtues and predispositions that would make it impossible to keep faith in the future.

All your thoughts, such as liking this and not that, are like

clouds that melt away in the sky. It is foolish to emphasize
your own thought that one thing is good and another bad
because all such thoughts, as well as their objects, quickly
disappear.

Visions and realizations are also impermanent, unless
you have attained the final ones. Although there are very
good as well as bad visions – sometimes so bad that anger
arises – you must understand that they do not last and try to
bring them to a state of voidness. Therefore, no matter how
clear or beautiful your visions are, you should not think that
they make you great. The point is to increase visions and
then finally to let them be absorbed in an extinguishment of
all conceptions. Therefore, do not be proud, but lead them
towards the Truth Body. Then death itself, which usually
seems so frightful, is not really so. Death will be a means of
returning home so that it will be a great pleasure to die.

The mind is both beyond death and blissful by nature,
and so are you if you realize its nature. You become like a
great eagle that swoops down to take its food and soars
away unimpeded. It does not fear anyone or anything. The
mind has been caught in cyclic existence, but as soon as we
have understood its nature we can transform wherever we
are into a pure land.

In our present state – unless we are just foolish – we have a
sense of sorrow about death. Mi-la-re-ba said, 'Why did I
go into retreat? Because I was afraid of death.' Fear arose
because he meditated night and day on the uncertainty of
the time and cause of death. Impelled by this, he sought the
primordial nature of his mind, and when he found it, he
overcame all fear of death. Does this mean he did not die? It
was necessary for his mind to separate from his body
because anyone with a body of flesh and blood eventually
has to abandon it. Yet, when Mi-la-re-ba's mind finally
separated from his body, he did not suffer at all.

Gam-bo-ba said that when you first begin to practise,
you must be like a deer locked in a pen or a prisoner in jail,
urgently seeking a way out. In the intermediate stages of

practice you should be like a farmer during the harvest. Once he has determined that it is time to reap his crop, he works at it continuously, no matter what anyone tells him. Just as a farmer works to make the most of the crop he has grown, so we who now have opportunities and conditions, which are so valuable to our practice, should use them immediately, understanding that there is no time to be wasted. In the final stages of practice you should be like someone whose work is drawing to a close and who is looking forward to the time when he can put it aside and live at ease.

With regard to how much time there is for practice, you should be like someone who has just been hit by an arrow and who is trying to get rid of it. He does not bother about who shot it or where it came from, he acts swiftly to remove it.

When you meditate, you should be like a mother who has lost her only child, but its image is with her whatever she is doing. Then, in the later stages of practice that are concerned with realizing emptiness – the final nature of all phenomena – you should be like a herdsman who has brought all his beasts home. He has had much to watch and cope with, but now they are all home safely, and he feels relaxed; his mind is freed.

If you repeatedly meditate on impermanence, attraction for the things of this life will be lessened, making it easy for Buddhas to bestow blessings on you. If you achieve great realization of impermanence, they will appear to you and foretell your future lives, including the one in which you will complete the path.

There are many types of meditation in Buddhism, and the best is impermanence. In the jungle the elephant has the biggest footprint, and in meditation the greatest mark or effect is left by meditating on impermanence. This is a great quintessential instruction. Whether you are going, wandering, lying down or sitting, you should keep this understanding of impermanence intact in your consciousness, never allowing your mind to lose it.

Buddha said, 'Even if you make marvellous offerings to the best in my own retinue – to the best of all monks – the merit thereby acquired would be only a tiny portion of that achieved by one moment of concentration on impermanence.'

A Ga-dam-ba Ge-shay was asked, 'Please explain the most important of all practices.'

He replied, 'That is meditation on impermanence.'

'Why is it so important?'

'In the beginning meditation on impermanence acts as the cause of entry into doctrine; in the middle as the cause of impelling practice; and in the end it generates realization of the sameness in nature of all phenomena.' He repeated this advice many times, 'Meditate on impermanence.'

In short, meditation on impermanence acts first as the cause of seeking the doctrine, then of practice, and finally of achievement. Bodhidharma[18] said that if you generate an understanding of impermanence in your mental continuum, it will ultimately release you into the clear light of your own mind.

What is the measure of having successfully generated a sense of impermanence? A Ga-dam-ba Ge-shay was staying in a small retreat on a hill. There was a thorn bush near the entrance, and whenever he walked through the door, the thorns ripped his clothing, and he thought, 'I must cut down this bush.' Yet inside his retreat he reflected, 'If I took the time I would spend cutting down thorns and used it to meditate, I would progress in understanding the nature of my mind and that would help me much more than a doorway without thorns.' So he did not cut down the bush. After his meditation session he went outside, and the thorns again tore his clothing. Once more he thought to cut them and again, for the same reason, did not. Eventually he became a great adept.

Please strive hard to reduce your attachment to all things in your present life because their appearances are temporary and so neither truly profound nor beneficial.

6 Faults of Cyclic Existence

We can determine with utter conviction and without much reasoning that we will all be dead in a hundred years.[12] Will death be like a fire going out or water evaporating? Not at all. This empty mind, which is happy and sad, not physical and not just nothing, cannot possibly end.

What happens to the mind if it does not die? Your own virtuous and non-virtuous actions determine what your mind will undergo during death and afterwards. The effects of these actions follow the mind like a flower and its scent. An act of anger can serve as a cause for rebirth as a hell-being, while one of desire can give rise to a hungry ghost, and another motivated by delusion can lead to rebirth as an animal. These three actions are the causes of birth in the three lower realms.

What is cyclic existence? It is like a potter's wheel or a water wheel. It can only go round and round in the same place. It is like a bee caught in a jar. No matter how much it flies round inside, all it can do is dart to the top, the middle, or the bottom of the jar. Cyclic existence is like the jar, and our mind is like the bee because whether we are born as a god, demigod, human, animal, hungry ghost or hell-being, we remain in cyclic existence.

We have been travelling in this round of rebirth since beginningless time. If it were agreeable to be born in cyclic existence, we could just relax and be happy because there is no end to it. However, its very nature is suffering.

Since we have been born in cyclic existence from time without beginning, there is no sentient being who has not been our own mother, father, brother, sister, best friend and so on. Nagarjuna said that if you made the whole earth into little pellets and let each one stand for a sentient being who has once been your mother, you would use up all the pellets before you could finish counting the mothers.[13]

When these beings were your parents in former lives, they were as kind to you as your own have been in this one. Among all those who are now friends, enemies, or neutral to you there is not one who has not nurtured you in her womb, given birth to you, and taken care of you as a small child.

Since desire, hatred, and ignorance cause birth into cyclic existence, the only way to become free is to eliminate your own desire, hatred and ignorance. You cannot overcome these without engaging in practice, and there is no way to do so if you do not have opportunities and conditions as a human being. Therefore, any sentient being who has provided you with an opportunity for human birth has been extremely kind, and these kind beings are in a miserable state. Let us consider their situation.

Thoughts about the individual sufferings of the six types of living beings begin with hell-beings. The eight hot hells are said to be arranged one on top of the other, and the suffering becomes stronger and stronger as you descend the levels. Each has its own land composed of burning-hot iron.

The first hell is called Reviving. Birth here results from having committed murder, and its inhabitants are people who have killed each other in the past. The moment they see their old enemies again, they pick up their weapons and strike each other. After they have all been killed, a voice from the sky commands, 'Revive, revive.' They rise and begin killing each other once more. Life in this hell consists of continuous repetition of this sequence.

How long does it last? Fifty human years is one day in the life of a god in the Heaven of the Four Great Royal Lineages. Three hundred and sixty of these days equals one year, five hundred of which equal one day in the Reviving Hell. A hell-being will live there five hundred such years.

What would it be like to be born in such a country and suffer so much?

The second hell is called Black Line. Here the servants of the lords of death arrange their victims like blocks to be cut – drawing four, eight, sixteen, or thirty-two lines on their bodies. A saw of burning-hot iron cuts along the lines. If someone sawed us in this way, we would die, but the past actions of the beings in this hell are such that they do not. They even retain all feeling in their severed limbs. These beings live even longer than those in Reviving Hell.

A hundred human years is one day in the life of a god in the Heaven of the Thirty-Three. One thousand such years equal one day in a Black Line Hell, and a hell-being there will live one thousand such years.

The third hell is called Crushed Together. Countless sentient beings are placed in a mortar of burning-hot iron, and a pestle the size of a mountain descends and crushes them. It is like squashing bugs except that as soon as the pestle is raised the beings come to life again. Their suffering seems endless.

How long does one remain there? Two hundred human years is one day in the life of a god in the Heaven Free of Combat, and two thousand such years equal one day in a Crushed Together Hell. Life there lasts two thousand such years.

The fourth hell is called Crying because those who are there are always wailing. It is a room of burning-hot iron with no doors or windows. There is no way out. It is filled with multitudes of sentient beings.

Four hundred human years is one day in the life of a god in the Joyous Heaven, and four thousand such years equal one day in a Crying Hell. The beings in it live four thousand such years.

In the fifth hell, Great Crying, there is another house made of burning-hot iron, with two rooms, one within the other. Because of its design, beings there have the additional fear that if they escape from the inner room they will only find themselves in the outer one.

> How long do these beings live? Eight hundred human years is one day in the life of a god in the Heaven of Liking Emanation, and eight thousand such years equal one day in a Great Crying Hell. Beings there live eight thousand such years.

The sixth hell is called Hot. It consists of a huge iron vessel as large as the thousand million worlds of a world system and filled with molten iron. The victims live in the molten iron, and as they boil up to the surface, the servants of the lord of death, who are created by the beings' own former deeds, grab their necks with an iron hook and beat their heads with an iron club.

> Sixteen hundred human years is one day in the life of a god in the Heaven called Controlling Others' Emanations, and sixteen thousand of these years equal one day in a Hot Hell. Hot Hell beings live sixteen thousand such years.

The seventh of the hot hells is called Very Hot and is also a house of burning-hot iron. The bodies of beings living there are riddled by three-pronged pitchforks wielded by the servants of the lords of death. These weapons, of burning-hot iron, are driven in through the heels and anus and up through the shoulders and head. The length of life of those here is so great that it cannot be measured, but is estimated to be half an intermediate aeon.

The last and the worst of the hells is called Most Tortuous. This is a house of burning-hot iron so hot that the sentient beings and fire become one. A bellows works steadily to increase the heat more and more. A life span there is one intermediate aeon.

What actions lead to rebirth in the Most Tortuous Hell? If you take tantric vows and then break them without trying to correct the transgression, you are born in Most

Tortuous, as is one who commits any of the five heinous deeds. The five are: (i) killing one's father, (ii) or mother, (iii) drawing blood from the body of a Buddha with evil intent, (iv) killing an Arhat, and (v) creating dissension in the spiritual community. Any of these will cause birth in the Most Tortuous Hell immediately after death.

After an intermediate aeon in Most Tortuous the person is able to leave, but only to pass through the Neighbouring Hells which stand at the four quarters: Burning Ashes, Mud of Corpses, Plain of Razors, and Grove of Swords. Between each of these are Iron Grater Hells.

When the karma or action that caused one to be reborn in the Most Tortuous Hell is finally spent, the person comes out. He sees in the distance a marvellous grey plain, so attractive that he immediately rushes toward it, but sinks into hot ashes.

Eventually he is released and sees a marvellous lake in the distance. He has gone for so many years without water that he rushes to it with great delight. On arrival, he sinks into a mass of rotten corpses – dead horses, cows, humans and so forth. In this mud of rotten corpses are animals with iron teeth that gnaw at his body.

Once more he is finally freed and sees in the distance a grassy plain. Delighted, he rushes to it, but finds it is not grass but razors. Wherever he steps, his foot is cut, but when he raises it, it is healed only to be cut again at the next step. Although the end of this plain seems to be near and in reach, it keeps receding due to his own past actions.

Eventually he is released from the Plain of Razors and sees a dark cool grove in the distance. He eagerly runs toward it, but when he gets there, the winds of his own past actions cause the sword-like leaves and branches to slash him as he passes.

Because one of the four Neighbouring Hells stands in each of the four cardinal directions, no matter by which side of the Most Tortuous Hell he leaves, he is bound for one of them. In passing from one to the next he comes across an

Iron Grater which is a great hill that looks wonderful. He looks up toward the peak and sees his best friend standing there. The friend says, 'I have not seen you for such a long time, please hurry and come on up!' He feels so happy to see his old friend. As he begins to ascend the hill, it changes into a grater, like that used for grating cheese, and his body is shredded as he ascends. When he finally reaches the top, the beautiful girl or marvellous fellow – the good friend – turns into a most horrible monster who bites his head and begins eating it. The victim glances down the hill, and there is his friend at the bottom, saying, 'Why are you up there? Come on down.' His body is shredded on the way down, and the great friend turns into a monster as soon as he reaches the bottom, again biting his head.

In meditation you should imagine that you yourself are undergoing these specific sufferings. You should imagine it to the point where a sense of fear is generated. Recognize that if you were in such a situation with the knowledge you now have, you would be terrified. Identifying the various types of sufferings that your own actions can induce will cause you to generate the effort necessary for attaining an understanding that makes it impossible to undergo suffering. You could then choose to be reborn in a hell without experiencing the slightest suffering.

Normally we are oblivious to others' pain, and this meditation is a way of becoming aware of the various sufferings that other sentient beings undergo. It can cause you to generate tremendous compassion for them. Furthermore, when you see the situations into which actions such as hatred will lead and when you comprehend the type of person that they make you become, you will be contrite for the acts of hatred done in the past. You will develop an intention not to become involved in afflictions in the future.

There are also eight cold hells. These are lands of snow and ice. Born in the first one, Blister, where the suffering is lightest, you suffer from cold blisters. Among the three types of feeling – pleasurable, neutral, and painful – you

experience only pain, and the suffering is very hard to bear.
Bodily strength fades, speaking becomes difficult, and your
breath is slow and laboured. In the next hell, called Bursting
Blister, it is even colder with the result that the blisters crack
and burst. The third cold hell, Chattering, is colder still so
that your teeth chatter. The fourth is called Moaning,
because you make a sound like 'Ahoo ahoo ahoo'. The next
is called Groaning. Here your body has become so weak
that you cannot make as loud a noise as in the Moaning Hell,
but utter a gasp that sounds like 'Gehoo gehoo gehoo
gehoo'.

The sixth is so cold that the blisters split, with the flesh
cracking open like a blue lotus. In the seventh the body is
said to split like a red lotus because the skin opens all the
more and the red inner flesh is exposed. In the coldest hell,
the body is split into eight, sixteen, or thirty-two parts, like
a large red lotus, and small animals with iron teeth gnaw at
the exposed flesh.

Beings in these cold hells live for an inconceivable length
of time. If every hundred years someone took one seed out
of a storeroom filled with two hundred bushels of sesame
seed, the length of time needed to empty the storeroom
would be the life span of a being in the first of the eight cold
hells. In each subsequent hell the span is twenty times
longer than the preceding. During your meditation session
imagine that you are undergoing these specific sufferings.
Take time actually to experience the sufferings of each of
the eight cold hells. This will give you the impetus to seek a
way beyond suffering, not just for yourself but for all
others.

There are also Lesser Hells that can occur even here in the
human realm. For example, after death a consciousness may
enter a tree because it mistakenly believes that its body is
one. When the tree is chopped, it seems that this is
happening to its own body. If a consciousness mistakenly
thinks it is a pestle, whenever the pestle is used to grind
spices, the person feels that his own body is being crushed.

Sometimes people think they are brooms, and they feel considerable pain when they are swept across the floor. Another may think he is a pot, and when he is put on a stove, he feels that he is being burnt. Some believe their body is a door, and whenever that is opened or closed they feel they have been beaten. Some believe they are pillars, feeling compelled to remain in one spot for many years and support a ceiling. For those who think they are cords or ropes, there is the pain of being pulled, stretched, twisted and so forth.

There is a famous story about a lesser hell that took place in a lake. A great yogi approached the lake and began to cry. When the people with him asked why he was crying he told them it was because he saw that a monk, who in his previous life became rich through deception, had been reborn there. Through his occult powers, the yogi then made it possible for the others to see what he saw. Instead of water they saw a fish-like monster whose body was as large as the lake itself. Little animals, fish and so forth, were eating its flesh. They were people who had been cheated by the monk in the past.

Another lama sent a group of monks to a river, telling them to bring back everything that floated by during the day. They saw nothing but a log, which they brought to him. They split it open, and inside was a being who had managed a monastery with great malevolence in the past; he was being eaten by an enormous number of minute sentient beings. There is also a story about a householder who lived in India at the time of Buddha. He took a layman's vow saying, 'I cannot keep from killing during the day, but I will not kill at night.' He lived accordingly and, when he died, was reborn as a very beautiful woman who had four servants during the night. At daybreak his mansion turned into a filthy hovel, the four servants became beasts and the woman herself a monster.

Shrona, who was learning to moderate the tightness and looseness of his mind as mentioned before, was travelling

round India and came upon a monastery inhabited by many
excellent monks. He wanted to eat with them, but instead of
offering Shrona food they urged him to leave. Shrona
pretended to go but hid where he could see and hear them.
At noon when the monks were supposed to be eating, their
begging bowls were transformed into weapons, and they all
leaped up and began beating one another. After the meal
they again became excellent monks and went about their
duties as usual. Shrona returned and asked the cause of their
strange behaviour. He was told that long ago in previous
lives they were monks under the Buddha Kashyapa and had
begun fighting during the noon meal, and this was the cause
of their midday transformation.

Why do we talk about the different hells? It is to lessen
attachment to the appearances of cyclic existence. Once you
know the sufferings entailed and these strike your mind
forcefully, your understanding will motivate you to search
out a way to avoid suffering in any situation. You may feel
there are certain objects for which you cannot overcome
attachment, but this is the result of being overcome by the
present moment's temporary happiness. This happiness
will soon leave and eventually turn into suffering. Therefore, the point is to cultivate in meditation a sense of the
range of possible sufferings so as to overcome attachment to
present appearances. It may not be possible to remember all
types of suffering in detail, but at least you can recall the
names of the different hells and generate a sense of the pain
that beings born there have to undergo.

7 Suffering

Meditation on the faults of cyclic existence is an important step in a long series of practices which can eventually enable you to understand the highest view, called the 'essential purity'.[14] The path for realizing this is called 'breakthrough', but before you can tread it successfully you need to experience the practices that reveal the range of conscious experience.

Pride is one of the chief faults that prevent people from advancing in their practice. If you are unable to sense the sufferings of cyclic existence, you will not know your limitations and your pride will grow as your knowledge and skill do. If you are able to generate a sense of the sufferings in the three lower realms, then it will be impossible to develop pride in your own good qualities or fortune. You will know that you are still susceptible to such horror.

A very proud monk came to visit a lama, who asked him, 'What do you know?'

'A great deal,' he replied, 'I know a great many books.'

The lama then asked, 'What are the eighteen hells?' The monk recited the names of the eight hot and eight cold hells, but he could not recall those called Neighbouring and Lesser. The names of two cities came to his mind, so he gave them instead. Being too proud to say he did not remember, he lied.

After hell-beings, the most unfortunate type of rebirth is that amongst hungry ghosts. They may live in their own realm or roam in our world. In general they suffer most from hunger and thirst. There are two types. The first are born in very poor and depressed areas where almost nothing grows. They may search for food and water for hundreds of years without finding a scrap to eat or a drop to drink. If they spot a stream in the distance, by the time they reach it it has always dried up. If they see an orchard, when they come near, it turns out to have neither fruit nor leaves. To add to their troubles, in summer they suffer greatly from cold and in winter from heat.

The second type of hungry ghosts suffer from physical deformities. Some have large bodies but throats like the eye of a needle, and legs too weak and skinny to support them. Even a tiny scrap of food which they swallow burns when it reaches their stomachs. Others, because of past misdeeds, besides being always hungry and thirsty, have parasites feeding on them.

These special sufferings come in many forms. Shrona once visited a city of hungry ghosts where he met a beautiful woman sitting on a throne, the legs of which were four hungry ghosts. Because Shrona was a monk, the woman offered him a generous meal but asked him not to give any to the hungry ghosts. When he started to eat, they began to beg, until he finally gave a little food to each of them. As soon as it reached the hand of the first hungry ghost, it became a piece of hot iron that seared his flesh. The next one raised the morsel to his mouth but found he was eating his own hand. For the third it turned into hay, which he ate, and for the fourth it became pus and blood.

Seeing this, the woman said, 'I told you, Arya Shrona, not to feed these hungry ghosts. You have no more compassion for them than I do. All this is due to their own past actions.'

Shrona asked, 'Please tell me how they came to be this way.'

She pointed to the hungry ghosts one by one and said, 'This was my husband, that my father, this was my mother and that my son's wife in my last life. We all lived together, and one day a monk came to our house. I asked them all to offer him food, but they wanted it for themselves, and so they cursed him. My husband said, "Why don't you give him a piece of iron to eat?"; my father, "Give him some hay"; my mother, "Give him pus and blood," and my daughter-in-law said, "Let him eat his own hand." I fed him and made a wish to be reborn in a position to witness what my family would undergo as a result of their misdeeds. And so I was born in this way with them as my servants.'

The hungry ghost who had been the daughter-in-law then asked Shrona to find her daughter, who had become a whore in one of the Indian cities, and tell her of her mother's fate. She then requested him to take the gold and silver that still remained in their old home and offer it to the monks in the area while dedicating this virtue to the eventual enlightenment of all sentient beings. In this way she wished to cleanse the bad relationship between her family and the monk who had begged them for food.

ANIMALS

The animal realm, the best of the three bad realms, refers to animals living in the sea and on land. Those in the watery depths are especially prone to the suffering of the larger eating the smaller and the smaller latching onto the bodies of the larger and eating holes in them. Those on land suffer particularly from being used by others.

The worst affliction of animals is stupidity, for they are so dull that even though they are being used or about to be eaten by other beings they cannot free themselves. Their minds are so obscured that they do not know what to do and what to avoid; they have no notion of how to engage in religious practice.

There are many examples of how animals are used by

other people and deprived of all freedom. Sheep are kept for their wool; when sheared, they may be injured, but they have no choice. Others, such as tigers and bears, are killed for their skins, elephants for their tusks and musk deer for their musk. Their own bodies have led to their deaths.

Animals are so tortured with endless suffering that they seem to be drunk with it. Their distress is caused by former actions motivated by ignorance, confusion and obscuration. In meditation you should imagine that you yourself are undergoing all this, and you will wish to gain such understanding that you will never again have to suffer such pain.

HUMANS

You may feel that although beings born in the three lower realms have many horrible sufferings, we for the most part enjoy comfortable conditions. In reality, however, humans, demigods and gods do not have even a moment of happiness. Humans are subject to the three great root sufferings and their four great currents.

The first of the three great root sufferings is that of change. This means that although we carry on as if there were a great deal of happiness in marriage and in seeing friends and so forth, we are unable to keep this happiness, as it turns into suffering almost immediately. For instance, there are many people who have married only to have their happiness ruined by an adventitious circumstance such as an accident. We cook to please our friends, and then, due to their own condition, this food – meant to bring pleasure – brings great sickness. Rich people often suddenly become destitute through chance happenings such as theft or fire.

The second great root suffering is a double dose. It is a case where one type, such as the death of a parent, is followed by another, such as illness. This is called suffering on top of suffering.

The third great root suffering is called that of conditioning. Our life situation is such that we are always ready to suffer. When we are happy, it may seem that our life is completely without misery, but the seeds thereof are always present, and we are capable of experiencing pain as soon as the appropriate conditions arise.

Furthermore, our happiness usually involves a non-virtuous activity that itself is a cause of misery. For instance, a condition of our sitting down to enjoy a good chicken dinner is that someone had to kill the chicken. We must understand that even things which appear to be pleasurable are actually suffering in that our involvement with them will cause us to suffer in the future.

The four great currents of suffering to which humans are subjected are birth, ageing, sickness and death. In our world there are four types of birth: from a womb, an egg, heat and moisture, and spontaneous.

Birth from a womb, which we know best, takes place when a being from an intermediate state (*bar-do*) enters into the drop of the semen of the father and the blood of the mother in the womb. The intermediate state occurs between two lifetimes, and a being there does not have a body composed of flesh and blood but only a mental one. Because a bardo-being knows that this state can bring great suffering, it frequents places where animals and humans are copulating in hope of finding a good place to be reborn. Its mere proximity, however, does not determine its form of rebirth. If it is a bardo-being whose past actions determine that it is to be reborn as a human, then even if it encounters copulating dogs, it cannot enter into the womb of a bitch. Only if the winds of its own actions impel it there, can it enter a canine or any other womb.

If it is to be reborn as a human, it will eventually come to a place where a couple is copulating. If it is to be a male, it will experience a great liking for the mother, and for the father if it is to be a female. The winds of its own actions force it into the centre of the drop of semen and blood that has gathered in the female's womb.

Once the bardo-being's consciousness has entered this drop, it becomes fixed there and cannot leave. After the first week, its suffering begins. It feels that it is powerless and trapped in a very dark, dull place, so close that it feels choked. In the second week the foetus is in a jelly-like state, in the third it hardens, and in the fourth week it grows longer. Its shape is now mainly that of a human head, and as it develops into a more elongated state, its features become clearer.

The time that the baby spends in the womb is difficult for both mother and child. The mother may experience different illnesses depending on the condition of her body, and whenever she is sick, the child suffers a lot. It is hard for her to carry the child as it grows larger and larger, and it is unpleasant for the child to stay so long in such a foul-smelling place. Whenever she drinks or eats something hot, the child experiences extreme heat, and when she takes anything cold, experiences extreme cold. Sometimes when the mother sits down, it feels squeezed, or when she stands up, as if it is being crushed between two rocks.

After about nine months a wind arises, turning the child upside down in preparation for birth. The master Padmasambhava said that at the time of birth a mother feels she has taken a long step toward death. For the child, the experience is like being forced through a narrow iron opening. Afterwards, no matter how smooth or soft a cushion he is laid upon, he feels as though he has been put on a bed of thorns. Hence, once he is born there is nothing he can do but cry, and his crying is a sign that the suffering is more than he can bear.

Ageing is the second of the four great currents of suffering. The hair turns white and old age spots appear on the face. The physical force decreases, and food once easily digested is no longer so. All these are signs of the suffering of ageing. When your teeth fall out and you who were once so beautiful lose your energy, you are left with the thought, 'Oh, I have become so old.' But, even people who no longer care for the life they live are fearful of death.

Our bodies are composed of earth, water, fire and wind and have the three humours of bile, phlegm and wind. When these components are out of balance, we become sick. Then even courageous people who are willing to rush off to war at a moment's notice will just lie on their backs and moan. At such a time a proud and domineering person has neither pride nor domination; he is reduced to almost nothing.

When we are sick, we are uncomfortable night and day. We who previously ate only the finest food now have to take a most unappetizing medicine, and a surgeon may have to cut up our insides. Our surroundings become dark as if the sun were setting, and we are so weak that demons may enter us. If we have a contagious disease, our friends avoid us, and we are left alone. Although our breath is still moving back and forth, we feel that we are seeing our own corpse. We become a little crazy, thereby adding more suffering to what was already great misery.

After a while even the nurses may ignore our requests, and we become angry and depressed. Even if we do retain power over those around us, we are unable to improve our own condition. We realize that we will have to be reborn, and if we have not practised any religious discipline, we have the further sadness of knowing that because we have not cultivated virtue, we will very likely be reborn as an animal, hungry ghost or hell-being. Friends come round and ask us what is wrong or how we feel, but they cannot share our illness. We have to bear it entirely alone. Although we are too ill to use or enjoy possessions, our attachment to what we have increases. Yet, no matter how wealthy we are we cannot take with us even a needle and thread.

Often when a sick person senses that the messengers of the Lord of Death are approaching him, a special uncontrollable fear is generated. When he understands that he is about to die, he looks into his mind to see if anything there can protect him from suffering. His sense of regret may be so great that he claws at his own chest in grief. Watching the death of a sinner can be a great teacher, causing you to understand the effects of harming others and stimulating effort towards altruistic practice.

Do not think that the hot and cold hells are far away or that going there requires a great deal of travel. When you begin to die, your mind experiences those hells right here.

The rich suffer from the fear that a thief may take away their wealth, and most of us dread meeting a hateful enemy, who may appear suddenly at any time, interrupting whatever happiness we have.

We all have the fault of being attached to our friends and alienated from our enemies. Yet, no matter how close we are to our friends, we cannot stay with them forever. Moreover, the feelings of closeness and alienation that we have for others create in our minds bad influences which loving friends cannot share – we must carry them all ourselves.

All of us are the same in wanting happiness and not suffering. Despite the fact that we seek happiness so eagerly, it is extremely difficult for us to attain as much of it as we would like. We build a house hoping to be happy, but it falls down. We engage in commerce to amass wealth, but a thief takes it and leaves us beggars. We suffer from being unable to carry out our wishes, and when these are unfulfilled, our desire for happiness becomes yet another cause of suffering.

Although we often cannot attain what we want, we frequently get what we do not wish for. We want one thing and are left with its opposite. This applies to all sentient beings because all have this problem of getting the unwanted.

Couples want to stay together forever, but the partners have to die, separating from each other. Even people who want nothing more than to hear teachings from their own lama must leave him eventually, just as everyone must finally part from their friends and carry on alone. Because all such happiness ends in separation, the renowned Nying-ma-ba Lama Jik-may-ling-ba said, 'Now is the time to make preparation; now is the time to practise in order to achieve the great happiness from which you can never be separated. I would not waste my time saying this to people who were not discouraged with the sufferings of cyclic existence. I speak for the sake of urging you away from that existence and onto the proper path.'

DEMIGODS

Demigods are motivated mainly by jealousy. Fights and quarrels break out among them as soon as they are born. Although they fight among themselves, their main adversaries are the gods, whose realm is situated directly above their own. The gods receive whatever they want from the branches of a wish-granting tree. But the roots and trunk are in the land of the demigods, who are very jealous because the gods, and not themselves, enjoy the fruit. Aroused by jealousy, they wage war on the gods.

When this happens, the gods, whose nature is such that they never become angry, go to a grove and drink from a lake created by water flowing out of a monster's mouth. This enables them to become angry so that they seize armour and return to repulse the demigods. The heads of state go to war seated on the thirteen heads of an elephant, with Indra, chief of the gods, in the middle.

Because the gods have more merit than the demigods, they are able to jump and fly much higher; thus they have a great advantage. If a demigod is wounded, he is liable to die, but the gods can only be slain if their heads are cut off. The wounds that a god receives are immediately healed by a special nectar that appears as soon as he has been hurt. This difficult warfare, motivated by jealousy, is the particular suffering of demigods.

GODS

Gods enjoy the greatest happiness, comfort and prosperity
in cyclic existence. However, they are so addicted to their
prosperity and comfort that they never think of practising.
Their very long lifetime eventually ends, and in the days
preceding their death they suffer greatly as they see how
they are about to be reborn.

Five signs indicate that death is near. The vast sphere of
light that they usually emanate begins to shrink and dim.
Their former comfort and delight in the environment fades,
and they become dissatisfied. Flowers and garlands, which
remained fresh and beautiful throughout their life, now
begin to wilt, and their clothes, which have been clean and
new, now become dirty and full of holes. For the first time
they begin to sweat, and by all these signs they know that
they are dying. All their friends and family also know it;
they cast flowers from a distance and make a wish that the
dying god may be reborn as a human, engage in virtue, and
thereby be born again into a realm of gods in the future.

The dying god clairvoyantly sees where he is to be reborn.
He knows that he will separate from the great fortune of
gods, leave friends behind, and be reborn in far harsher
conditions than those to which he has become accustomed –
most likely in one of the lower realms where he will suffer
hunger, thirst, heat and cold. His distress as he perceives the
future is very great, and he has to endure it for seven
god-days, equivalent to seven hundred human years. In our
terms this would be like undergoing the same type of
suffering in rebirth after rebirth, through seven centuries.

If you understand the suffering of gods, you will not be
attached to their apparent happiness. The master Nagarjuna
said in his *Friendly Letter* to King Shatavahana that even the
great gods Brahma and Indra would ultimately die and take
rebirth in one of the three lower realms. Therefore, he
advised the king not to be attached to the great prosperity of
gods.

If it is unsuitable to be attached to the wealth of gods, then it is certainly the same with regard to other types of happiness within cyclic existence. Padmasambhava said that to live here is like living on the point of a needle. There is no happiness in it. You should understand that no matter where you are born you will not find even one instant of happiness. If you make urgent effort to understand this in meditation, you will gradually lose your attachment to worldly appearances.

Buddha had a young cousin named Nanda whom he was encouraging to become a monk, but Nanda was very attached to his wife. Buddha took him to a temple and used many means to turn his mind towards doctrine, but the young man could not bear to stay there and ran home. Buddha, being clairvoyant, knew that he was leaving and met him on the path. As they walked on together, they came across a very ugly and repulsive hag so hideous she was without any beauty whatsoever.

Buddha said, 'How would you compare your wife with this woman?'

Nanda answered, 'My wife is at least a hundred thousand times more beautiful than she is.'

Buddha then said, 'Would you like to visit a realm of the gods?'

Nanda said, 'Yes,' and was transported by Buddha's magical powers to a realm of gods. He saw many beautiful houses where groups of gods and goddesses were living in great comfort. One of the houses was inhabited only by goddesses. There were no gods, and the ladies were sitting here and there as if they were waiting for someone.

'Why are you here alone without companions?' he asked them.

'There is a young man named Nanda, Buddha's younger cousin, who will be reborn here with us as a result of his good ethics.'

Nanda then went running back to Buddha, who asked him, 'Did you see the country of the gods?'

'Yes, I did.'

'Who was more beautiful, your wife or those goddesses?'

'Just as there was a difference between that repulsive beggar and my wife, so there is an even greater one between my wife and those goddesses.'

'Are you capable of keeping good ethics now?'

'Yes, I am.'

From that time, Nanda kept excellent ethics, thinking all the while that by doing so he would be reborn near those lovely goddesses. Such a motivation is not the basis for true ethics, and therefore Buddha, with his great skilful means, announced to a gathering of monks that because his cousin was keeping ethics for the sake of rebirth as a god, the other monks who were doing so in order to attain Buddhahood should not keep company with him. He cautioned them that although their behaviour looked the same from the outside, their inner thought was vastly different, and therefore he urged the other monks not to eat or talk with Nanda.

Nanda was sad at being left alone and could not understand why, since his ethics were still good, the others would have nothing to do with him. He consulted Ananda who explained that his poor motivation was the reason why he was not permitted to stay with the rest.

Nanda sadly returned to his solitary room and was again approached by Buddha who this time offered to use his special powers to let his cousin visit a hell. Nanda went and saw a great vessel in which many sentient beings were being boiled. He saw another one surrounded by the workers of the lords of death but it was empty. Nanda inquired, 'What is the purpose of this vessel?'

'There is a fellow named Nanda,' they answered, 'who will be reborn among the gods because of his good ethics. His life will be long, but his merit will be consumed, and not having engaged in new virtue, he will eventually die and be reborn here. We are preparing this for him.' Nanda was very frightened and ran back to Buddha. From then on, he was able to keep excellent pure ethics with the motivation of attaining complete liberation from cyclic existence rather than just from the lower realms. With pure ethics as his basis, he meditated, penetrated the process of cyclic existence, and became an Arhat.

8   Cause and Effect of Actions

What cause the sufferings of cyclic existence?[15] Our own actions. Pleasure is produced from virtuous acts, and suffering from non-virtuous ones. In general, there are ten non-virtuous actions to be refrained from at all times and ten virtuous ones to be adopted in all ways.

The three physical non-virtues are killing, stealing, and sexual misconduct. The four verbal ones are lying, divisive talk, harsh words and senseless speech; and the three mental ones are covetousness, harmful intent and wrong views.

The vilest of all non-virtues is killing. Whether its force is strong or weak depends on the presence or absence of four factors:

   (i)   identifying the sentient being who is the victim
  (ii)   forming an intention to kill
 (iii)   engaging in a means of killing
 (iv)   causing the life faculty to cease.

The worst form of killing occurs when all four factors are present; it has the greatest force to create future suffering for the murderer. If, for example, a man aimed to kill a particular person but missed his mark and slayed someone else, the first factor of having identified the actual victim would not apply even though it would indeed be very wrong to have killed another person.

Stealing can be done in three ways, by authority, robbery

and deceit. The first refers, for instance, to a king who forces his subjects to pay more tax than is due. It also applies to anyone who uses coercion to pressure others into giving him what he should not be getting. The second way of stealing is through robbery, using stealth to take what is not given. The third type comes through deceit and occurs frequently in commerce. Merchants often charge more than their goods are worth in order to get as much out of the customer as possible. Among traders the tendency to steal through deceit is very strong.

Commerce, in general, is an all-consuming activity. There was a trading monk on whose doorstep the great yogi Mi-la-re-ba once slept. The monk was inside, lying on his bed and making plans to kill his cow the following day. He spent the whole night thinking about the different prices he would receive for its various parts, counting so much for the skin, the head, the legs and even the tail. Finally, at sunrise he got up, did his morning recitation, made his offerings and breakfasted – his thought all the while on the commerce of the day. As he was leaving the house, he saw Mi-la-re-ba still sleeping beside the door, and said, 'What is wrong with you? Can you not see that the sun has risen? You are supposed to be a practitioner; get up and get busy.'

Mi-la-re-ba answered, 'I usually rise very early to practise, but I have a cow that I am going to kill, and I spent all night thinking about the money that I will make from it.' The monk was very embarrassed and fled in shame.

There is tremendous fault in spending time thinking about the profit that you can achieve through commerce. Just as the monk was so busy thinking about it that he had no time to sleep, so it is extremely difficult for anyone engaged in commerce to have time to meditate. You have so many figures to add and decisions to make about what articles you can sell for maximum profit that you have no time for practice.

The third physical non-virtue is sexual misconduct, and regarding this there are two codes, one for householders and the other for monks. For the former it is permissible for husband and wife to rely on one another, but to use prostitutes – especially through the medium of pimps – is a great carnal sin. If a husband or wife has taken a vow to abstain from sexual activity for that day, it is wrong for the spouse who has not done so to use the one who has. It is also improper to use one's wife if she is sick, menstruating, about to have a child, or during the month following childbirth. It is also improper during a time of great grief, such as just after a parent has died. This act in a library or in front of an image, such as in a temple, is also sexual misconduct. It is wrong for a man to take a girl whose parents are keeping her very closely, or one who is not yet ripened, such as a girl of ten or twelve. The main principle in all of these constraints is not to force other people to engage in sex against their will. It should be pleasurable for both.

The fourth non-virtue – the first of the four verbal ones – is lying. This includes ordinary lies, great lies and lies of vanity. An example of the first would be to praise your own possessions beyond their worth for the sake of gaining respect or a higher price. Great lies consist of, for instance, denying that non-virtuous actions have any effects, or saying that pleasure does not arise from virtue, or that Pure Lands or Buddhahood do not exist. Because there are no lies more erroneous than these, they are called great. A lie of vanity occurs when someone who has not attained any grounds or paths boasts and pretends that he has clairvoyance or has seen a spirit or deity.

Second among the verbal non-virtues is divisive talk, which can be either open or hidden. To accuse a person of harming another in his presence is an instance of the open kind. Hidden divisive talk is to approach someone and tell him that a certain person has been abusing him, without the accused person's knowing anything about your allegation. The worst of all such talk is that which creates a division among people practising doctrine.

The third verbal non-virtue is harsh words. This often comes in the form of unkind names or mockery, such as calling someone a one-eyed blind man because he is partially sightless, or someone a robber who is not. We never know who among us is a Bodhisattva; thus, if we speak harshly to anyone, we may be abusing a Bodhisattva, and this is the worst of all harsh speech.

Senseless speech means talking about fighting, wars or other senseless things. It is extremely disruptive for someone who is meditating to do so. He will not find the time for what he set out to accomplish.

The eighth, ninth, and tenth non-virtues are mental, and the first of them is covetousness. It is very easy to develop this, especially in large stores. You may see a beautiful watch and find yourself thinking, 'May I have this?' Or you may notice beautiful clothing and think, 'I must have it.' This is covetousness. It is similar to desire but involves specifically a yearning for something that is not your own, whereas desire can apply to either your own or others' possessions.

Harmful intent is a wish to hurt others, for example, plotting to make a rich man lose his wealth, or cause a very bright one to fail in his studies.

Wrong views are the heaviest of non-virtues because they are instances of having inverted opinions about vital topics. There are 360 wrong views which can all be included within the categories of permanence and nihilism. For example, the belief that cause and effect do not exist would be a view of nihilism.

The effect that arises from a non-virtuous action can be of four types. The first is a fructification effect; this means that the deed bears fruit as a whole life in one of the lower realms. Such deeds are like stones that are thrown only to plummet downwards. Any non-virtuous action motivated by hatred will inevitably cause rebirth in a hell. One inspired by desire causes rebirth as a hungry ghost, and one by obscuration leads to rebirth as an animal. It is also said that a non-virtue motivated by strong hatred will cause rebirth in a hell, one inspired by middling hatred as a hungry ghost, and one by weak hatred as an animal. The same is true of actions motivated by strong, middling and weak desire or ignorance. When you are impelled into one of the lower realms, you will undergo the effects of your action until its power is consumed.

The second type of effect is similar to its cause. Here, instead of being impelled into a whole lifetime in a bad migration, you experience a similar type of effect. The similarity can be a likeness of either function or experience. An effect similar in function is a case in which someone has killed in the past and is therefore predisposed to do so even more. As a little child, such a person would take delight in killing bugs and small animals. Likewise, someone who stole in the past might have an affinity for continuing to steal. If you wonder what you did in previous lives, look at your body; its size, shape and features have been determined by your past actions. If you wonder where you will be born in the future, look at your present activities for they will decide your next life. Even in animals we can see instances of effects of similar function; the various birds and beasts that like to kill one another are cases of beings who liked doing so in their previous lives.

With regard to an effect of similar experience, let me give an example. As a result of having killed someone through hatred, you would be reborn in a hell, but if the force of your action had not been entirely consumed during that rebirth, you might then be reborn as a human who would be murdered or who would die on the day of his birth. As another example, a robber in a former life might be a frequent victim in this one, or lose his wealth in a fire.

Therefore, the best way to ensure good resources in the future is to stop stealing and engage in giving. There are people in our world who gave much in their youth and later – even in the same life – attained many resources as a result. These are instances of effects similar in experience.

The effect of sexual misconduct is to have an ugly and highly unpleasant spouse. This misconduct can also cause your family life to deteriorate within the same lifetime. You may think that your husband or wife quarrels with you because it is his or her natural disposition to do so, but actually the effects of your own former actions are ripening into a temporary manifestation.

If you lie, you will be slandered by others who do not recognize your value, education and qualities, and who only spread lies about you. If you make divisions among people, the effect similar to the cause will be that your companions will fight with you constantly and there will be many people who do not care to be your friend.

As an effect of harsh words, you will be put in a position where you must hear many such words about yourself, and even if you speak honestly to others, they will quarrel with you. Speaking harshly is a very heavy non-virtue, and its effect can last for several lifetimes. Although words are not weapons, they can cut another's heart. Harsh words are motivated by hatred, and when any non-virtue is involved with hatred, it becomes extremely heavy. If we speak harshly about very special beings such as Buddhas or Bodhisattvas, the bad effects will last for many lifetimes.

The Brahmin teacher Kapila, the greatest of the Hindu debators at the time of Buddha, was sent out by his mother while the Buddhist monks were on their begging rounds. She wanted Kapila to debate with them because she felt he was such a great scholar that he would overcome them in debate. There were eighteen monks and to each of them he called out a bad name, 'Hey, horse-head. Hey, ox-head. Hey, dog-head,' and so on. The monks thought he must be someone of no or very little virtue and, therefore, felt they should not debate with him. This made him all the more proud, and he called them stupid and shouted that they knew nothing.

Soon after this Kapila died and was reborn as a fish in the Ganges. He was so big that when some fishermen caught

him in their net, his weight pulled them all into the water.
Many others then gathered together to pull him in, and
when they laid him on the bank, they saw that he was a sea
monster with eighteen heads.

They asked Buddha to bless him, and in doing so Buddha
empowered the fish to talk. The monster told them that he
was formerly the Brahmin Kapila. Buddha asked him,
'What action caused you to be born this way?' The fish
answered that it was because he had shouted foul names at
eighteen monks.

This was the occasion when Buddha first taught confession, the revealing of one's own non-virtue. It begins with
an obeisance to the thirty-five Buddhas and includes a
revelation to them of all misdeeds. The monks recited this
formula with the fish monster who, because of his great
belief, was able to overcome the effect of his name calling.
He died and was reborn in one of the abodes of the Gods, the
Heaven of the Thirty-Three.

Do not feel it is ever appropriate to call anyone a bad
name. The person may seem ordinary, but you have no way
of knowing he is not a Bodhisattva. During the time of the
Buddha Kashyapa, a monk called another one a bitch, and
the effect of this was that he was reborn as a dog 500 times.
How do we know this? Buddhas are so clairvoyant that
everything appears to them as clearly as if it were in the
palm of their hand.

It is told in scripture that some of Buddha's audience did
not believe a word he said, and a Buddhist layman and a
non-Buddhist finally decided to test him in order to find out
if he really was clairvoyant or merely inventive. For their
experiment they collected grains and wrote down which
farmers had grown each of them. They also burned pieces of
wood and wrapped up the ashes, noting down from where
they had been cut. The samples were put into vessels which
they buried in the ground.

They then asked Buddha to identify what was there and
to describe the origins of each. Buddha identified the grains

and told them the grower of each and from which of his fields it had come. With the ashes, he identified the specific tree from which the wood had been cut. There were 500 samples in all, and Buddha was able to describe each flawlessly. 'Since my understanding is limitless, I could take one little piece of dust and tell you endless stories about it,' he said.

A Buddha's consciousness has been so transformed that he is able to know the phenomena in all world systems as clearly as we would see an olive in our own hand. To speak harsh words to such a being, or to Bodhisattvas who are on the verge of becoming Buddhas, is particularly harmful because it means you are deprecating these magnificent qualities, or even claiming that they do not exist. Through claiming that there are no such attainments you cut yourself off from the possibility of developing them; thus the effects are very heavy.

Any act of hatred can immediately turn the mind in a bad direction; one toward higher beings can extinguish the meritorious power that has been accumulated for a hundred or even a thousand aeons. If a first ground Bodhisattva becomes angry for one moment at another such Bodhisattva, one hundred aeons' accumulation of virtuous power is lost. If a Bodhisattva becomes angry at a higher one, one thousand aeons of virtuous power is lost. Thus there can be no doubt that even among common beings anger does inconceivable harm to the mind.

If you talk divisively, the effect of similar function will be that your mind is so disturbed by hatred that you will be deceived out of your own goodness. Through senseless talk your speech will have no force to attract others' attention. No matter how interesting the subject is, no one will care to hear about it from you. No matter how clear and straight-forward you are, people will doubt your words.

The effect of covetousness is an inability to complete what you have set out to accomplish. As a result of harmful intent it becomes very hard to gain friends, and through wrong views you will have great difficulty in generating faith.

The third type of effect is environmental. Here, the effects of actions manifest as the environment into which you are born. If you kill, you may be reborn in an extremely ugly area where it is difficult to sustain life. As an environmental effect of stealing you might live on land such that even though you planted excellent seeds, you could not harvest a good crop. Famine would come to the area, and starvation would be extremely hard to avoid. As a result of sexual misconduct you would be born in a foul-smelling and rotten area.

Through lying, the environmental resources necessary for existence become completely unreliable. Divisive talk can cause rebirth in a land where it is difficult to accomplish tasks directly, and by speaking harsh words you are cast into a very rough place with dangerous cliffs and frightening forests. Senseless talk has the effect of making it very difficult to grow a meaningful crop, and it brings on a confusion of events such as rain needed in the spring falling during the winter.

The environmental effect of covetousness is birth in an area where the situation does not accord with your own thoughts and wishes. As a result of harmful intent you are born in a place where you must always wonder about being killed. Through wrong views you come to live in an area where teachers, friends, and protectors are very difficult to find.

The fourth type of effect that an action can have is a cumulative effect. This is a case of one sin leading to more and more. Because the sinful activity itself is increased, it is sometimes necessary to pass through many lifetimes before becoming free of an affinity for that non-virtue.

Just as there are ten non-virtuous actions to be abandoned, there are ten virtuous ones to be adopted. In general, engaging in the ten virtues consists of making a very strong promise to desist from the non-virtues and practise their opposites. It is sufficient to make such a promise by yourself, but it is stronger if you do so in the presence of a special object such as a lama or an image of Buddha. If you are in a situation where it is necessary to kill bugs in your home or animals to eat, any amount by which you can decrease the killing is good. That much at least is an improvement. If it is not possible for you to keep the ten virtues all the time, keep them on special days, especially when the moon is full and new.

There was a butcher in India who was unable to stop killing during the day but vowed that he would not slaughter at night. As a result, he spent the days of his next life in a lesser hell, staying in a burning iron house with four hideous women. The effect of his successfully sustained vow not to kill at night was that after dark his iron house turned into a marvellous mansion and his companions became four lovely women.

The effects of virtues are the opposite of those arising from non-virtues. Through practising the former you are born in a fortunate realm with good resources and excellent friends, in a situation conducive to practice. Through virtue you are able to take rebirth as a human, to continue practice and further your understanding until you are able to free yourself from cyclic existence completely.

Through desisting from killing and by protecting life you will enjoy a long life free of disease. Through forsaking stealing and practising giving, you will ultimately attain good resources. By abandoning sexual misconduct and maintaining good ethics you will have a loyal and likable mate. If you stop lying and speak the truth, you will hear the truth as well as praise of yourself. When you avoid divisive talk and speak harmoniously, you create the causes for meeting with compatible, friendly and helpful companions. When you abandon harsh words and speak lovingly, others come to speak in the same way, and you do not have to hear harsh words. When you refrain from senseless talk and speak with meaning, your own speech becomes clever.

Through desisting from covetousness and cultivating admiration and delight, you become always able to achieve what you wish. By avoiding harmful intent and becoming helpful, others will assist you. By giving up wrong views you find it easy to cultivate right ones.

When you engage in virtue, your own virtuous power increases and leads you to practise still more virtue so that you become a person of great meritorious power.

Everything within cyclic existence – from its uppermost peaks to the depths of its hells – is created by our own actions and the predispositions they establish. No matter how powerful, wealthy or fortunate anyone is, he can only enjoy these fruits temporarily because the force of his good actions runs out. In sutra it is said that no matter what one has done, the effect is certain to arise, be it within the same lifetime or aeons later.

All the varieties of sentient beings are due to their different actions in the past. Each birth is influenced by one's own predispositions, as are the events of one's life. Buddha's disciple Maudgalyayana was capable of great magical feats, and yet he was severely beaten by others whom he had harmed in the past. Nagarjuna lived six hundred years, but King Shatavahana's son cut off his head with a blade of grass because in a former life Nagarjuna had killed a worm in the same way.

A Kashmiri monk who was clairvoyant and had many magical powers was in a forest, boiling a red liquid to dye his robes. A herdsman who had lost his calf saw the smoke and approached, wondering if it might be in the pot. When he looked, the robe appeared to him as a calf; so he accused the monk of having stolen and butchered his calf. When the monk looked into the pot, he also saw a calf. The herdsman brought him before the king, who put the monk in jail.

In time the herdsman found his calf and returned to the king to tell him that the monk could not have stolen it, and the king decided to set him free. However, during the next six months the king was so busy that he did not find time to see that the monk was actually set free. Finally the monk's students, who also had magical powers, flew into the presence of the king and told him that their teacher should be let out of jail. The king immediately went to fetch him and found that he was near death. 'I have committed a great sin,' said the king, and berated himself for his neglect.

The monk told him there was no need for remorse because he had incurred this treatment through his own bad actions in the past. The king was amazed and asked, 'What did you do that bore such terrible fruit?'

'In a former life I was a robber and stole a calf from a herdsman, who saw and pursued me. I ran until I came upon a yogi meditating in the forest, put the calf down by him and ran away. The herdsman soon reached the yogi and, when he saw the calf there, assumed that the yogi had stolen it. As a result the yogi was put in jail. I caused him a great deal of misery, and had to suffer for it in a hell, but when I left the hell, a little of the force of the action still remained, so I had to suffer from it again in this lifetime.'

If such special people as this clairvoyant monk have to undergo the effects of their own former actions, what need is there to say anything about ordinary people like ourselves?

Shantideva says that one moment of non-virtue can cause rebirth in the most tortuous hell for an aeon.[16] We are all people who have sinned from time without beginning, so it is clear that we will have to suffer a great deal as a result. The *Sutra of the Wise Man and the Fool* (*Damamūkonāmasūtra*) says that one should never feel that even a tiny non-virtue will bring no harm. Its effect can be very great, just as a tiny spark can set fire to a whole mountain of hay.

A tiny virtue can also have great power to bring about immense happiness. A little boy happened to see one of the Buddhas who preceded Shakyamuni Buddha, and he was so happy that he threw him a handful of peas. Four of them landed in the Buddha's bowl, and as a result, the boy was reborn as a universal monarch with control over four continents.

It is very important to realize that the effects of virtuous and non-virtuous thoughts and wishes can be extremely powerful. Even if a person appears to be engaging in virtue, if his motivation is evil, the effect will be very bad. Therefore, it is necessary to be mindful at all times and aware of your motivation and thoughts. In this way, if your mind is carried away by bad thoughts or poor motivation, you will be able to stop them.

How should such mindfulness and introspection be used? A Ga-dam-ba Ge-shay[17] was expecting a visit from his patrons, so he rose early and made his house very beautiful, cleaning it well and attractively arranging offerings on his altar. When he had finished, he sat on his meditation cushion and revived his mindfulness and introspection to analyse what he had just been doing. Very quickly he understood that his cleaning and arranging had been motivated by a desire for praise and a wish to receive further donations from his patrons.

He rose, took a handful of dirt, and sprinkled it everywhere – on top of the offerings, into the water in the bowls, and over the floor. Then he sat down again on his meditation cushion and beat his breast, 'Oh monk, do not be so careless. You must take care.'

The arriving patrons were surprised to hear the loud noise and to find the house in such chaos. 'What is wrong?' they asked. 'Did a robber come?'

The Ge-shay told them, 'The robber that made this mess was not physical but mental.'

The great Indian teacher Bodhidharma[18] was visiting Tibet at this time and when, through his clairvoyance, he realized what the Ga-dam-ba Ge-shay had done, he said, 'There is no better practitioner of doctrine in Tibet than he. He covered with dirt the head of the being who threatened to draw him down into a bad rebirth.'

The same Ga-dam-ba Ge-shay once came to recite

religious books at the home of his patrons, who went out
after he had finished, leaving a container of tea bricks within
reach of where he sat. In his own meditation hut he had no
such tea, so it occurred to him to take one while the others
were outside. As he was reaching for it, his mindfulness and
introspection returned, and he immediately began shout-
ing, 'Robber, robber.'

The patrons came running into the room. 'Where is he?
Where is the robber?'

'A monk is robbing you; it is my own hand. Would you
kindly cut it off?'

Indeed, it is very difficult for ordinary people not to have
unworthy thoughts, but the most important point is not to
be carried away by them when they arise and, through
mindfulness and introspection, to avoid becoming stuck in
them. By being always mindful and introspective, you can
develop the superior view, and your own behaviour will be
without blemish.

Guru Padmasambhava taught meditation to the Tibetan
King Tri-song-day-dzen (*Khri-srong-lde-brtsan*) and gave
this advice, 'In my Secret Mantra teaching, the profound
view is most important, but it is absolutely necessary to
behave well in addition.'

What is the fault of having an apparently profound view
without good behaviour? In the early stages of practising
the view when you are trying to pass beyond good and bad,
it is easy to behave badly because you are predisposed to do
so. When you lose your mindful understanding of the view,
the residual bad behaviour is ready to manifest. Then, when
practising good behaviour, it is necessary to remember that
all the factors involved are not inherently existent. If you
think that these factors so exist, you will be tightening the
noose that binds you to cyclic existence.

Mi-la-re-ba's students became convinced that he must be
an emanation of the great Vajradhara because of his
excellent qualities, and they asked him to confirm this.
Mi-la-re-ba told them, 'You may think you are flattering

me, but from the point of view of doctrine there is no greater insult than what you have said. I am an ordinary being who learned black magic and through it raised a hailstorm that caused my uncle's house to collapse and kill him. When I gained conviction in the cause and effects of actions, I understood that this deed would result in birth in a very unfortunate realm. Deeply contrite for my misdeed, I entered the path of doctrine, relied on my teacher, received quintessential instructions, practised in accordance with them and achieved their objects. Living alone in the mountains I was able to become an actual Vajradhara. If you practise as I did, you also will be able to become Vajradharas.'

Because they have not ascertained the cause and effect of actions, people do not practise. For anyone who does ascertain this, the entry into practice is easy.

9 Benefits of Liberation and Reliance on a Spiritual Guide

Liberation is the state of freedom from all sufferings in cyclic existence.[19] There are three types of liberation: those of a Hearer (*Shrāvaka*), a Solitary Realizer (*Pratyekabuddha*) and a Buddha. Your own meditation and practice can become the extraordinary and marvellous cause of Buddhahood itself. Therefore, once you determine that liberation exists, you should engage in its causes.

The foundation of all practice is the four reversals: the difficulty of attaining opportunities and conditions, the impermanence of life, the faults of cyclic existence and the cause and effect of actions. The first two turn the mind away from achieving only the affairs of this life, the last two from achieving only the welfare of future lives. Internalizing these provides the basis for effective practice by reversing your mind from the temporary appearances of cyclic existence. Through causing it to accord with these practices, your mind will become serviceable, flexible and capable of practice. In this way the root of the path leading to the omniscience of Buddhahood is established.

The preparatory practices are like one wing of a bird, the actual ones are like the second wing. With two wings a bird can fly, and with these two sets of practices your own mind can be transformed.

Buddhahood can be attained only through a union of method and wisdom. The practice consists of abandoning non-virtue and maintaining virtue as well as cultivating the four immeasurables of equanimity, love, compassion and joy. These are the foundation. Of the paths themselves, the most significant are those of calm abiding (*shamatha*) and special insight (*vipashyanā*). Through a union of these one is able to advance on the path. It can also be said that progress is made possible through a union of all six perfections: giving, ethics, patience, effort, concentration and wisdom.

The first five perfections must all be conjoined with wisdom, and there are two ways of understanding the relationship of the other perfections with wisdom. Giving, ethics, patience, effort and concentration can be practised in the context of the wisdom realizing the non-inherent existence of the factors of agent, action and object. These five perfections can also be seen as causal qualities that make wisdom possible. There is no contradiction here. It is impossible to complete the perfection of wisdom unless you have made progress in achieving the five preceding ones. Also, if you have any of the five perfections but do not have wisdom it is impossible to escape from cyclic existence or attain Buddhahood.

The fifth perfection, that of concentration, is the practice of calm abiding which is the mental factor of stabilization. The practice of special insight is included in the perfection of wisdom, and it enables you to sever the root error that causes the fall into cyclic existence. The wisdom of special insight understands the space-like nature of phenomena. When the stabilizing factor of calm abiding is attained, it is conjoined with this realization of emptiness. In this way it is possible to sustain your understanding in long meditation.

The *Condensed Perfection of Wisdom Sutra* (*Sañchayagāthā-prajñāpāramitā*) says that wisdom must be generated even before engaging in giving and the other perfections. According to this sutra, if your giving is not conjoined with a wisdom consciousness which understands that none of the factors of giving can be found under analysis, then your action will be a mere giving and not a perfection of giving.

You must understand that giver, giving, gift and recipient do not exist inherently in and of themselves – that they are empty of objective existence. Wisdom seals each of the other five practices as perfections; thus there is no way to perfect giving, ethics, patience, effort or concentration unless they are conjoined with the wisdom realizing their emptiness. Without this, they will never lead to Buddhahood. Wisdom itself is beyond thought, inexpressible, transcendent, not produced and not ceasing. It is like the very entity of the sky – the mother of all Buddhas of all times.

Before coming to rely on a spiritual guide who can teach such a path it is necessary to analyse him. If this shows that he is a suitable guide, the second step is to develop skill in relying on him. The third step is to train your mind in the lama's thoughts and deeds.

The initial analysis made by a prospective student is extremely important and should be done with great attention. In this degenerate era it is very easy to confuse true lamas with impostors. We ourselves are full of afflictions, and lamas who deceive their students with artifice do occasionally appear. A true lama, however, would either not know how to deceive or would find it utterly unthinkable to do so. Unless you analyse a lama well, you may come to rely on a false teacher. This would be like mistaking poison for food, so take care. To take poison by mistake is a waste of this precious life, but reliance on a deceitful teacher can ruin many lives.

A true lama is like a channel through which the blessings of all Buddhas flow. For this reason, once he has been chosen, it is necessary to regard him as a being of total purity. It is your thought of him as extremely pure that creates the possibility of his blessings entering into and empowering your mind. You should rely on your teacher the way a bee receives honey from a flower, taking the best that is there, taking just what it needs and then returning to its home. The bee does not become involved with other aspects of the flower. You should learn to take from the lama those qualities which he or she has as if they were being poured from one vessel into another. Once you have received these good qualities of mind, return to your own place. We have a saying that when it comes to incense or a lama, one should keep one's distance. Incense smells very pleasant from a little way off, but if you get too close, the smoke will enter your nose and make your eyes water. If you stay with your lama day in and day out, you will inevitably begin to find fault with him and by so doing become incapable of receiving his blessings and help.

The three ways to delight a lama are to serve him, to give him things and, most importantly, to achieve what he teaches. When training in his thought, try to determine what his altruistic mind, love and compassion are. The supreme goal of this training is to develop a determination to seek enlightenment for the sake of others – induced by love and compassion for all sentient beings.

Naropa was an outstanding scholar in Nalanda monastery, but he had not yet learned what it meant to rely on a spiritual guide. Arya Tara appeared and told him that he must seek out a teacher and rely on him. 'Your teacher's name is Tilopa and he lives in eastern India. Go and search for him; he has been your guru for many lifetimes.' Hearing this, Naropa resigned his abbacy, handed the monastery over to other monks, and set out for the east, taking only his monk's robe, staff and begging bowl. He wandered about eastern India asking after the guru Tilopa, but no one had heard of him. Then he began inquiring about someone called Tilopa, without mentioning that he was a guru. Finally a man pointed and said, 'There is a beggar named Tilopa living in that broken-down hut.' Naropa reflected that gurus quite often show themselves as persons other than teachers, so he approached the beggar's hut.

Tilopa was seated in front of a fire, and at his side was a pail of live fish, which he was taking one by one and placing on the fire. After a few moments he would pick one up, snap the fingers of his other hand, and eat it. Then he would put the next on the fire. Naropa approached him and bowed down. 'Please take me under your care.' Tilopa turned his back and continued to fry and eat the fish. Naropa approached from the other side, bowed down and repeated his request. Tilopa turned round and continued. Naropa made a great effort, bowing down many times and repeatedly asking Tilopa please to take him under his care.

Finally Tilopa answered, 'All right.'

What was Tilopa doing with the fish? He was a highly accomplished yogi and had the power to lead these beings out of their animal state and establish them in a higher rebirth. Other great adepts, such as Saraha, also were able to direct a sentient being's mind to a higher life and sometimes even disguised themselves as hunters to do so. To our common sight it is appalling to come upon adepts who are acting as hunters or frying fish alive. However, once a lama has been analysed and accepted as your own teacher, you must view his activities with pure perception. His extraordinary powers are often not accessible to our understanding. The marvellous story of Naropa's following Tilopa is a measure of how great the effects of such trust can be.

After their meeting in the beggarly hut, Tilopa took Naropa with him everywhere but did not teach a word of doctrine. They came to a nine-storey house, and Tilopa said, 'If somebody really wanted to practise, he would climb to the top of that house and jump off.' Naropa looked round and he could see that there was no one else nearby to whom Tilopa could be referring, so he went to the top of the house and jumped off. As a result he broke many bones, suffered great distress and finally fell unconscious. Tilopa left him there for several days in great pain and just when Naropa felt he was about to die, Tilopa came by and asked, 'Oh, my son, are you sick?'

'Never mind being sick, I am nearly dead,' answered Naropa. Then Tilopa massaged him and his body was restored as before, due to the healing power of his teacher's hands.

Another time Tilopa asked Naropa to cut and collect many sharp splinters of bamboo and make a fire with them. Then Tilopa told him, 'If I had a real student, someone who truly intended to practise, he would take these hot pieces of bamboo and slide them under his fingernails.' Naropa did so until he fainted from the pain. When he came to his senses again, his lama was gone and his suffering was very great. Some days later Tilopa returned and asked as before, 'Are you ill, my son?'

'Never mind being ill, I am nearly dead.' Then Tilopa pulled out the bamboo splinters from under his student's nails and through his blessings Naropa's fingers were restored as before.

They went on from day to day until Tilopa handed Naropa his begging bowl, which was made from a skull, and asked him to find food because he was hungry. Naropa went to a group of woodcutters who were preparing noodle soup and asked for a cup of it. They agreed and filled the skull half full with their soup. Naropa brought it back to his teacher, and Tilopa acted as though he was extremely delighted with it. Seeing this, Naropa thought that if the soup so pleased his teacher, he should go and get him another cupful. He returned to the woodcutters' campfire and found that they had gone, leaving the pot behind. Naropa lifted the top and saw there was a little soup left, which he poured into his skull bowl. At that moment the woodcutters returned and when they saw him taking their soup, they beat him senseless. After a few days Tilopa came and asked him, 'Are you ill, my son?' and received the answer, 'Never mind being ill, I am almost dead.' Through Tilopa's empowerment, Naropa's body was again restored.

Naropa went through twelve such episodes; after each Tilopa came to him, asked if he was ill and then restored him to health. After this there were twelve lesser hardships. Tilopa put his student through these difficulties in order to clear away Naropa's karmic obstructions. Then one day he asked Naropa to boil water for tea and while the latter was kindling the fire, Tilopa grabbed him by the hair, took his shoe and hit him hard on the head. Naropa swooned, but when he regained consciousness he possessed all Tilopa's profound realizations and great qualities. Naropa attained a realization of emptiness equal to his teacher's and this came about entirely through reliance on his lama, for Tilopa never explained one word of doctrine to him.

To our common sight it might appear that Tilopa and Naropa were just making each other suffer, whereas in fact they were involved in a very special relationship. Tilopa was a great adept, and Naropa as his student had tremendous faith and a very strong karmic connection with him. Thus when the appropriate moment came, it was possible for the teacher to transfer knowledge directly to his student.

Let me tell you another story. The Bodhisattva Always Crying (*Sadāprarudita*) felt it was imperative that he hear about the perfection of wisdom and he searched constantly in the hope of finding a spiritual guide who could teach it to him. He went to great cities and small villages, but he came upon no one who was able to tell him all about emptiness and convey the perfection of wisdom. As he rested by the roadside, he heard a voice from the sky saying, 'O son of good lineage, if you wish to hear about the perfection of wisdom, go east.' The Bodhisattva started off in that direction, but when he realized that he had not thought to ask how far east he must go, he felt extremely sad. However he went on and the same voice said, 'Continue east. Before too long you will find a teacher of the perfection of wisdom.'

Soon he was approaching the neighbourhood of the Bodhisattva Dharmodgata. He had heard about this teacher and wished to make an offering to him, but he had nothing. 'Should I go to his house directly or first look for something to give him?' he wondered. An emanation of Buddha appeared and said, 'Continue east a little further, and you will find your teacher.'

When he was able to see the roof of the Bodhisattva's house, he decided to sell his own body in order to acquire the money for making an offering, but no one wanted it. He stood in the street weeping, 'If no one will buy my body, I will have nothing to offer the Bodhisattva Dharmodgata.'

The great god Indra was aware of Always Crying's situation and in order to test him, Indra appeared in the form of a brahmin. 'I do not want to buy a man,' he said, 'but I need a human thigh bone to use as a sacrifice.' The Bodhisattva immediately fetched a knife, rested his leg on a low wall and tried to cut it off, but could not.

A merchant's daughter noticed this from her window and called out, 'Why are you bringing all this hardship on yourself? Are you crazy?'

'I am not,' the Bodhisattva told her, 'I am selling my thigh bone because I wish to make an offering to the Bodhisattva Dharmodgata so that he will teach me the perfection of wisdom.'

'What great benefit will there be if you hear about this perfection?'

'If I hear about the perfection of wisdom, I will be able to cognize emptiness; if I do so, I can become liberated from cyclic existence and attain the great brilliance of Buddhahood.'

'Do not cut off your thigh bone,' she said. 'Since there is so much value in hearing about the perfection of wisdom, I will give you many things that you can offer to the Bodhisattva Dharmodgata.'

Together they went to her parents' home, and when they heard how he was about to cut off his thigh bone to hear teaching on the perfection of wisdom, they promised to give him everything he might need. The daughter herself now wanted to hear the teaching; she asked if she could go with him and together they set off in a chariot accompanied by five hundred attendants.

When they came within sight of the house, the Bodhisattva could be seen in the distance, lecturing to a large number of people. Always Crying had such great faith in the Bodhisattva Dharmodgata that merely seeing his teacher from a distance caused him to generate the joy of the first concentration. When they reached him, they made many offerings and then Always Crying, the merchant's daughter, and their five hundred servants requested that he teach them the perfection of wisdom.

The Bodhisattva spoke to them about the benefits of hearing this perfection and then concluded his lecture. 'I am going into solitary retreat for seven years,' he said. 'If you can wait that long, I will teach you the perfection of wisdom when I return.' They were very happy. After living in cyclic existence for endless aeons, seven years seemed a very short time to wait.

When six years and fifty-one weeks had passed, they began to prepare for the Bodhisattva Dharmodgata's return. They cleaned the place where he would teach and added many auspicious decorations and ornaments, but unfriendly spirits in the area raised gusts of wind which created clouds of dust. In order to sweep away this dirt they needed water to lay on it, but there was none to be found. Seeing this, the Bodhisattva Always Crying cut a vein in his neck to draw blood to serve as moisture. The others followed his example and spread their blood over the whole area until it had turned red. Indra, who witnessed this, thought, 'Indeed if they are willing to go through so much simply to hear about the perfection of wisdom, I should help them,' so he approached them and asked, 'What help do you need?'

The Bodhisattva Always Crying answered, 'I need to attain Buddhahood.'

'I am sorry, I cannot help you with that. If you have need for any object, I can give it to you.'

Always Crying replied, 'I do not need any objects.' However, in order to be of some use Indra turned all the blood into red sandalwood and created a marvellous mansion out of it. The Bodhisattva Dharmodgata then rose from his meditative retreat and began to explain the perfection of wisdom. Immediately upon hearing him, Always Crying was able to enter into 100 different types of meditative stabilization.

Buddhas and Bodhisattvas of the past had to undergo great hardship in order to receive even a single stanza of doctrine. We may not be able to bear such hardship but we should have a mind that gladly undergoes whatever difficulties occur on the path of seeking doctrine.

PART TWO

Special Internal
Preparatory Practices

Khetsun Sangpo Rinbochay's commentary on the
second part of *The Sacred Word of Lama Gun-sang*

10 Refuge

Going for refuge to the Three Jewels – Buddha, his Doctrine and the Spiritual Community – is the foundation of all Buddhist paths.[20] The door of refuge is opened by faith.

Faith is of three types: clarity, desire to attain and knowledgeable conviction. If when you see an image or meet a teacher you are overwhelmed with a feeling of, 'Oh, how nice this is, how wonderful,' this is the faith of clarity; the mind is clear and receptive.

The desire to attain means wanting special qualities that you have heard about, such as the compassion, love and wisdom of Bodhisattvas. It can also signify a wish to be free from the sufferings of cyclic existence, or to engage in virtues and forsake non-virtues. Through learning about the qualities of Buddha, his Doctrine and the Spiritual Community you can come to generate a desire to attain them.

The faith of conviction is, for instance, the knowledge that the Three Jewels are a suitable source of refuge. It is the seed generating these excellent qualities. If you are bothered by doubt, it is like having a seed that has been burned; it can still sprout, but it cannot grow properly and its seeds will be black, like smoke. It is said in sutra that without faith of conviction it is very difficult to generate any auspicious qualities.

Faith is like a wheel, always ready to roll along the road; if you have it, you can make internal progress at any time. Faith is an inexhaustible treasure of good qualities. It is a vehicle carrying you along the path to omniscience, an outstretched hand drawing you to all good qualities.

The extent to which spiritual qualities can be internalized depends on your faith. If it is middling, so are the qualities developed; if immeasurable, so too will be your attainments.

Buddha's own servant who remained with him for so many years was not able to generate any of his master's qualities because he lacked faith. When you have great faith, its benefit remains no matter how far away you may be from Buddha or your lama.

It is said that if you have faith, Padmasambhava will sit by your door while you sleep. The tutor of the Fifth Dalai Lama once entered his pupil's room through the window. 'Why have you come in through the window?' the Dalai Lama asked.

'There was no other way because a Nying-ma-ba lama is sleeping at your door,' the tutor replied. He was referring to the Dalai Lama's strong faith in the Nying-ma-ba transmission.

For one who has faith, even the tooth of a dog can bring blessings. If someone cherishes it as the tooth of a Buddha – whether he has been deceived or is simply mistaken – he will receive as much benefit as if it actually was a Buddha's tooth.

A simple fellow with great faith visited Lhasa in order to see the image of Jo-wo Rin-bo-chay in the main temple. He saw the food offerings that others had made and thought they were meant to be eaten by the image – which he took to be an actual person – and himself. He helped himself to a small portion and mixed it with the butter from one of the lamps. A group of dogs then ran through the temple and made off with Jo-wo Rin-bo-chay's food, and the fellow was filled with admiration at the way the marvellous lama smiled calmly through it all. The wind began blowing through the doors and nearly snuffed out the butter lamps, and again the fellow marvelled at how the lama could simply sit and smile at it all. It occurred to him to circumambulate the temple of this wonderful lama, but first he took off his shoes and respectfully placed them in the begging bowl on the lama's lap.

While he was outside, the keeper of the temple passed by the altar and saw the shoes in the image's begging bowl. 'Ah, these dirty shoes,' he exclaimed and started to throw them away, but he was stopped by a command from the image, 'Leave them here.' When the foolish fellow returned and saw his shoes still in the begging bowl, he praised Jo-wo Rin-bo-chay. 'Oh, you are such a fine lama, you have kept my shoes for me. Please come and visit me,' he said to the image. 'I will kill a pig for you and heat up some beer; we will have a fine feast.'

Due to his good thought, the image answered, 'Yes, I will surely come.'

The fellow returned home and told his family that he had met a very great lama who had accepted an invitation to visit them. 'I do not know when he will come, so please look out for him,' he told them. One day his wife went to fetch water from a nearby spring and in it saw a reflection of the lama. She ran home and called her husband. 'Your visitor has come, but he has fallen into the water. Please go out and help him.'

The man rushed out to the spring and saw Jo-wo Rin-bo-chay. 'Oh, the great lama has fallen into the water,' he cried and jumped in without hesitation. He helped the lama out and exclaimed, 'You have had so much difficulty getting here. Please come with me and I will offer you meat and beer.'

On the way the lama stopped and said, 'I cannot go to a lay person's home, I must return to my temple,' and disappeared into a nearby rock. The fellow then set the meat and beer out before the rock, which displayed an image of Jo-wo Rin-bo-chay.

We in Tibet still make offerings at the spring, now called Jo-wo Spring, and the rock where these events took place. Even though a statue is itself incapable of appearing as a living being, it did so to this simple man on account of his great faith. If you have firm faith that a Buddha is in front of you, he will indeed appear before you immediately. If you have faith in Buddha, the Doctrine that he taught and the Spiritual Community, the door to refuge opens, and you are able to enter all the numerous paths that the teaching contains.

Refuge is of three types: those of a being of small, middling, or great capacity. A person of small capacity is motivated to take refuge because he is concerned and fearful of falling into one of the three lower realms as an animal, hungry ghost, or hell-being. He believes that the Three Jewels can protect him from such misfortune and therefore takes refuge in them from the depths of his heart. A person of middling capacity has concern and fear about being reborn in any form – good or bad – within cyclic existence. Because he believes that the Three Jewels can protect him from all six realms, he takes refuge in them from the depths of his heart.

The refuge of a person of great capacity is due to his concern for the cyclic existence and obstructions of all sentient beings everywhere. He believes that the Three Jewels have the power to help all sentient beings to abandon the obstructions preventing liberation from cyclic existence as well as those preventing omniscience. Believing that the Three Jewels can offer this help to all beings, he takes refuge in them from the depths of his heart.

What are the three refuges? The first is Buddha, the revealer of refuge, the Teacher who shows us what it is. The second is the Doctrine, which is the actual refuge, and the third is the Spiritual Community, the beings who help us to take refuge. This interpretation is common to all Buddhist vehicles.

According to the extraordinary uncommon teaching of Secret Mantra, one's lama is considered to be undifferentiable from Buddha himself. One also relies continuously on a personal deity and on the Sky Goers (*Dākiṇī*). The lama is the manifestation and composite of all activities of all Buddhas in the past, present and future. He is the student's connecting link with the actual Buddha. The personal deities are beings appearing in fierce form to tame trainees who cannot be disciplined through peaceful aspects. The Sky Goers are female beings who bestow a quick means of attaining Buddhahood.

The Mantra Vehicle, or quick path, also teaches that the channels in your own body are, in their purified aspect, Emanation Bodies and that the winds or energies that flow in these channels are capable of being purified as an Enjoyment Body. The seminal essence of your body is, in purified form, a Truth Body. When we identify the channels, winds and seminal drops respectively as the Three Bodies and take refuge in them, this is called a vajra refuge. A vajra is a diamond sceptre, symbolizing immutability. This refuge is immutable because nothing can destroy or overcome it. It is true, with no deception.

In preparatory tantric practice, refuge is taken in the natural mind of enlightenment which is endowed with three qualities – entity, nature and compassion. Entity is the wisdom of emptiness; nature is that of clarity; compassion is the all-pervasive wisdom. These three – entity, nature and compassion – are the final objects of attainment and you take refuge in them to attain them. This is called an effect refuge because it consists of going for refuge to the fully developed factors that you are striving to manifest in your own mind.

When taking refuge, consider yourself as an ordinary being, not yet imagining yourself to be a deity. Imagine that the room or area where you take refuge is made entirely of smooth and beautiful jewels. They are made not of stone but of light, and the field is like a Pure Land.

In the centre of this land, in front of you, is a wish-granting tree made of clear light and capable of bestowing anything you might want. The trunk spreads out into five branches, each covered with the most exquisite leaves and flowers, in between which colourful ornaments sparkle. Hanging on the branches are large and small bells resounding through space. On the central branch are eight lions bearing a jewelled throne, upon which is a many-coloured lotus. On it are a sun and a moon, which serve as cushions, and Padmasambhava is seated on them. His nature is a composite of the minds of all Buddhas of the three times – past, present and future. His complexion is radiant like that of a youth, his skin white with a reddish glow. He appears in ordinary human form, with one head and two arms, and is seated in the royal posture – his left foot rests on his right thigh and his right leg is bent at the knee, so that his foot rests on the lotus cushion below. In his left hand, which rests in his lap above his left ankle, he holds a skull containing a golden vessel filled with the ambrosia of immortality and topped with flowers. If you are seeking peace or concentration, the flowers should be white; blue if you are training in a fierce manifestation, and yellow for vast activity.

Padmasambhava, who is called Guru Rin-bo-chay, wears a white inner robe and a blue silk garment beneath his religious robes, which are of red silk with gold brocade. On his head is a red and gold pandita's hat with two gold-trimmed visors folded up along his temples. On the peak of the hat is a golden half-vajra. The consort seated on his lap is the Sky Goer Ye-shay-tso-gyel (*Ye-shes-mtsho-ryal*).

Above their heads, seated on lotus cushions, are the lamas of the transmission that teaches the Heart Essence of Vast Openness, the Great Perfection. The topmost figure is Samantabhadra, the Truth Body, and below him is Vajrasattva, in the form of an Enjoyment Body. Third in the transmission is Ga-rap-dor-jay (*dGa'-rab-rdo-rje*), an Emanation Body; fourth is the teacher Manjushrimitra, fifth is the Knowledge Bearer Shrisimha and sixth is Jnanasutra.

Any lamas that you know personally can be visualized as seated beneath him, ending with your own fundamental lama. They are all sitting one above the other, with space between each. Amongst them are the protectors of Doctrine and your own personal deities.

To their right sits Shakyamuni Buddha, in the vajra posture. He is surrounded by the thousand Buddhas of this auspicious aeon, who are to be visualized in the form of Shakyamuni himself, seated in the same posture. Golden light emanates from them in all directions.

To the right of this group, which would be on your left as you face it, stand the protectors of the three lineages, Manjushri, Vajrapani and Avalokiteshvara, surrounded by tenth-ground Bodhisattvas. The three protectors are adorned with the magnificent ornaments of an Enjoyment Body. The Bodhisattvas are clothed in red monastic robes, and each carries a bowl and a staff in his right and left hand. Behind Padmasambhava and between these two groups are the traditional long, rectangular-shaped books of doctrine from which come voices teaching the subjects that each contains. To their left and right are male and female protectors, the former facing outwards to prevent all external interruptions and the latter inwards to prevent losing attainments already gained. Each of them is endowed with wisdom, compassion and power.

You come before this assemblage, facing it just above eye level. Your father stands on your right, your mother on your left and your worst enemy in front, facing the field of assembly. Other people, as numerous as the particles of earth in the world, gather behind and to the sides. All press their palms together in a gesture of respect, recite the refuge formula and petition the assembly to protect and aid your practice. All are stirred by faith nearly to the point of tears as you continually recite the refuge formula:[21]

> Until [manifesting] the essence of enlightenment I go for refuge
> To the actuality of the Three Jewels, the three sources [which are a composite of all] Sugatas

> To the mind of enlightenment which has the nature of the
>   channels, winds and drops [purified as the Three Bodies],
> And to the mandala of entity, nature and compassion.

Buddha, the Sugata who is the ultimate object of refuge, is
the actuality of the Three Jewels – Buddha, Doctrine and
Spiritual Community. The three sources are the lama (for
blessings), your own personal deity (for Siddhis), and the
Sky Goers (for special Bodhisattva activities).

In the sutra systems the natural mind of enlightenment
refers to the Tathagatha essence (*Tathāgatagarbha*), the seed
of Buddhahood present in all sentient beings. Here in
tantra, the natural mind of enlightenment refers to the
wisdom of clear light, the sole self-arisen drop of wisdom.
This mind is an undifferentiability of entity, nature and
compassion – respectively, the wisdom of emptiness, that
of clarity, and the all-pervasive wisdom of the union of
appearance and emptiness.

Refuge is usually recited six times daily, although some
repeat it much more often, eventually accumulating a
hundred thousand. This is helpful because it creates the
virtuous power necessary for the later practices. There is,
however, a shorter formula:

> *Namo*, I go for refuge to the Lama,
> I go for refuge to the Buddha,
> I go for refuge to the Doctrine,
> I go for refuge to the Supreme Community.

During meditation either formula can be recited while the
field of assembly is visualized. As you recite, pay respect
simultaneously with body, speech and mind. Physically,
respect is offered by bowing down to the assembly,
verbally through reciting the refuge formula, and mentally
by placing undivided confidence in the assembly with the
conviction that actual beings and not images are before you.

Before bowing down, put your palms together in the
shape of a lotus. Touch them to the crown of your head with
the thought that all your physical non-virtues are thereby

purified. Then place them at your throat to purify those of speech and finally at your heart for the mental ones. Then bow down. Slide your hands out in front of you and bring the palms together as before, stretching the body as much as possible. If you have not time for the full prostration, you can make an abbreviated one in which only the toes, knees, hands and head touch the ground. Repeat the refuge formula while you bow down.

At the end of each session, develop great faith as a result of which all the beings in the assembly emit rays of compassionate light. These rays enter your body and the bodies of those around you. Just as when a stone is thrown at a group of birds they immediately fly up, so when the light descends, you and the others are at once absorbed into it and drawn up into the field of assembly. The members, whose bodies are of light, then begin to melt from the outer edges into the centre until all dissolve into Padmasambhava. Then he, like a rainbow disappearing into space, dissolves into his heart, which melts away until it is the size of a mustard seed. And finally this small drop also vanishes.

Only empty space remains. Consider that your mind and that of each member of the assembly have thereby become undifferentiably mixed. Sustain this knowledge in space-like meditative equipoise as long as you can. When it is time to rise from meditation, the field of assembly, yourself and the other beings all suddenly reappear. Think of yourself and all activities as a magician's illusions. Finally, dedicate the merit of taking refuge to the welfare of each and every sentient being throughout space. Afterwards, continue to think of yourself and whatever you see or imagine as magical illusions, which appear and function but have no inherent existence.

In order to overcome obstructions caused by non-virtues, your practice should be conjoined with four powers. The first is the power of a special object which is the field of assembly itself. The second is that of contrition, which is your sense of regret for all the physical, verbal and mental non-virtue you have done from time without beginning. The third is the power of restraining your faulty behaviour by promising in the presence of these very special beings that henceforth you will not engage in physical, verbal or mental non-virtue. The fourth is that of the performance, which in this case is the obeisance itself.

After taking refuge, you should cease to view worldly deities as final sources of refuge, stop harming others, both manifestly and in dream, and no longer mix with evil companions. These three activities are to be forsaken from the time of taking refuge in the Three Jewels.

There are also three activities to be assumed. Having taken refuge in Buddha, you should respect even the smallest image of a Buddha as if it were him and consider it a means of purifying your faith. Having taken refuge in the Doctrine, you should consider any scrap of paper with a portion of the teaching on it as the actual Doctrine and view it with a pure mind. After taking refuge in the Spiritual Community, you should practise pure perception even of a piece of cloth from the robe of a member of that Community.

Further, the mind of the lama who teaches you is to be considered as the mind of Buddha, his teaching as the Doctrine and his body as the Spiritual Community. These are the three concordant practices of refuge.

If you are capable of taking refuge in the Three Jewels as you fall asleep, you should imagine the field of assembly within your heart. If you cannot do that, think of the members on your pillow. As you walk about during the day, imagine them sitting on your right shoulder; as you eat, that they are in your throat and that the food is an offering to them. If you are about to put on new clothing, hold it out and pretend that you are offering it to each member of the field of assembly. If you come upon a bed of flowers, feel that you are offering all of them to the assembly. Such activities are very virtuous.

Take refuge in the Three Jewels six times during the day,

three in the morning and again in the evening. These are excellent practices for keeping refuge in the forefront of your mind. Why is this so important? A lay practitioner in India was approached by his enemy, who threatened, 'If you do not stop reciting the refuge, I will kill you. If you stop, I will let you live.'

The practitioner answered, 'I will stop the verbal recitation, but not the mental one. You can kill me if you like.' He was slain on the spot and reborn in the Heaven of the Thirty-Three.

Because refuge is important and brings so much progress to beginners like ourselves, it was taught repeatedly in Tibet. One teacher who was adept in many other practices taught it so often that he was called the Refuge Pandita.

Buddha himself foretold that he would appear in the form of the letters of the refuge formula, and if you practise pure perception of the words of Doctrine, this can serve as respecting an Emanation Body itself.

The benefits of taking refuge are very great. In Tibet, a robber once broke into the cave of a recluse meditating alone in the mountains. It was late at night and there were no lights, so the robber felt round the room carefully to find what he might steal. The yogi waited quietly until he was approached and then grabbed the robber's arm and beat him over the head, reciting refuge and striking him once for each line, 'I take refuge in the Buddha, I take refuge in the Doctrine, I take refuge in the Spiritual Community.' Then the yogi let him go. It was raining and the robber ran to take shelter under a bridge. He thought it was very fortunate that there were only three places of refuge so that he had only been struck three times. He went over the whole scene again in his mind and began to recite the formula himself. A number of spirits who wished to kill him were passing over the bridge just then, but when they heard him repeating refuge, they were frightened and fled without harming him.

If merely repeating the words of refuge is effective, the

benefit from doing so with deep faith is very much greater. It is said in sutra that there is more benefit in taking refuge in the Three Jewels than in offering a whole world system of precious substances to a Buddha. Refuge opens the door to the practice of Buddhism and acts as the foundation of all advancement on the path of practice.

11 Mind of Enlightenment

The mind of enlightenment is the generation of an altruistic aspiration to highest enlightenment for the sake of all sentient beings.[22] It means that you have decided to strive for Buddhahood because you understand that only as a Buddha will you be able to care for and help all other sentient beings to escape the sufferings of cyclic existence and become Buddhas themselves. This practice has three elements: training in the attitudes of the four immeasurables, generating an altruistic aspiration to highest enlightenment and the precepts for so doing.

In the great books, the order of the four immeasurables is usually given as love, compassion, joy and equanimity. Here, however, the four are explained from the point of view of practice so that equanimity comes first. Why begin with this rather than love? It is a quintessential instruction passed down from the many previous lamas of this lineage that without the even-mindedness of equanimity it is impossible to generate love and compassion.

Before we can correctly identify equanimity, we must recognize that we do not have it for people around us. We are biased by love for our friends and hatred for our enemies, whereas one who has equanimity values both equally without generating desire or hatred for either. Looking inside our own minds, it is easy to see that we are deeply attached to some people and very hostile to others.

Yet, if we think about it, we will find that there is no reason to harbour such extreme feelings.

Since beginningless time we have been reborn in many different ways; an enemy today could easily have been our father, mother, son, daughter or closest friend in a previous life. For example, the clairvoyant Arya, Katyayana, when on his begging rounds came upon a young mother with an infant son on her lap. She was eating a piece of fish which a dog was trying to take from her, and she threw a stone at it. Through his clairvoyance the Arya knew that the fish had been her father in its former life and the dog her mother. She did not know her parents had been so reborn and felt no sympathy or affection for them. Moreover, the child she was cuddling had been a great enemy who had murdered her in her previous life.

This illustrates the changes wrought by rebirth in cyclic existence. There is no definiteness in our relationships with others because friends and enemies are constantly changing. Thus we should neutralize desire and hatred and free ourselves from bias, but this does not mean to enhance the indifference we have for people we do not know. That type of neutrality is not equanimity, but the result of not paying attention to certain people because they do not interest us. It is an equanimity of ignorance and desertion, not of the four immeasurables that leads to compassion.

In order to develop equanimity, visualize two persons, one liked and the other disliked, and meditate to discover whether you can equalize your feelings towards them. Another method is to imagine an enemy in front of you, your father on your right and mother on your left, and try to become even-minded about them. When you are able to equalize your feeling for these persons, practise it towards more and more people until you can consider all sentient beings without desiring or hating them on the basis of whether they are your friends or enemies. Because this equanimity encompasses all beings everywhere, it is immeasurable. In order to develop it, you must begin with specific individuals, not a generality.

Feeling uniformly about others is not sufficient; it is necessary to develop strong and equal love for each one of them. Just as a mother loves her child – caring for it, nourishing it, helping it develop – so should we have a love that seeks benefit for all sentient beings. Just as parents are willing to endure great suffering in bringing up their child, so must we be willing to make a great effort for the sake of these beings who are as limitless as space itself. Shantideva says that every sentient being should be seen with eyes of love.[23] If anyone asks us a question, we should answer in accordance with our knowledge, without impatience or anger and with as much love and joy as possible.

If you succeed in generating immeasurable equanimity, it will be easy to develop a sustaining love for all sentient beings. In cultivating love, you should reflect day and night, 'How can I possibly develop immeasurable love and friendship for all individuals?' To do so, picture the person you care for most and sense the sustaining love that you have for him. Then imagine someone else and show the same sense of sustaining love to her. One by one increase the number of those who are objects of your sustaining love until you can include all beings in all world systems. They want happiness but do not know how to cause it. They do not want suffering but do not know how to relieve themselves of it. What they wish for and what they do are at cross-purposes.

When the cultivation of immeasurable love grows strong, you will develop a spontaneous wish that these beings be free from suffering and its causes. Thus this love becomes a cause of great compassion, the third of the four immeasurables. To generate such compassion, think of the sufferings that others undergo. Imagine an animal or a human who is about to be killed, going to the butcher or the hangman, and pretend it is you. Consider how much suffering the knowledge of your own imminent death would cause, what feelings you would have just before being struck by the knife or having the rope put round your neck.

At other times consider that the one who suffers so dreadfully is your mother or father, and generate a sense of compassion and mercy by reflecting on that fact. If it were a member of your own family who was about to be killed, you would be deeply involved in trying to help him. No matter how little time remained before their death, you would use it to scheme how they might be spared.

Meditate on the suffering of others until you are ready to cry. First take individual cases and finally include all sentient beings everywhere because each and every one of them has been your mother and father in a former life and has suffered accordingly. The compassion you generate is a sense of not being able to bear their distress without doing something to relieve it.

Having developed compassion for the sufferings of sentient beings, generate joy for their happiness and good fortune now and in the future. Take as your object someone who is very wealthy or especially happy. Joy is the antithesis of jealousy; it is an inner delight at the good fortune of others.

When you have developed joy over one person, think how nice it would be if two or three more could be equally fortunate. Extend this sense of not being jealous and of rejoicing to more and more people until it includes everyone throughout space.

Once you have developed equanimity, love, compassion and joy, these will cause the mind of enlightenment to arise. This altruistic mind can be brought about in three ways. A person who realizes that before he can establish others in Buddhahood, he must attain it himself is said to have the mind of enlightenment of a king. One who is motivated by the thought that all other sentient beings will attain Buddhahood along with him has the mind of enlightenment of a boatman, because when the latter takes people across a river they all reach the opposite shore together. The third type of motivation is like that of a shepherd, who watches over his flock, keeps them out of danger, chases away their enemies and follows behind to make sure they all arrive home. Anyone so motivated will make sure that all beings attain Buddhahood before he does so himself. Of these three motivations, the weakest is that of a king, that of a boatman is next and that of a shepherd is unparalleled.

The mind of enlightenment is of two types, conventional and ultimate, the former being divided into the aspirational and the practical. For example, if you want to visit another country, this is an aspiration or wish to do so but not the actual going; similarly, if you have the desire to bring about the welfare of all sentient beings throughout space, you have an aspirational mind of enlightenment. Once you have generated this aspiration so that it is spontaneous and begin to practise giving, ethics, patience, effort, concentration and wisdom for the sake of sentient beings, then you have a practical mind of enlightenment. This is like actually going to another country.

The meditational technique here is to imagine a wish-fulfilling tree and the field of assembly in front of you as when taking refuge. Consider the very special beings in that field as witnesses of your intention. Make the promise to concentrate on achieving the highest enlightenment for the sake of others from this point on. Do this with the intense hope that whatever portion of the mind of enlightenment has not arisen in any other sentient being will be generated and that whatever has arisen will greatly increase. Recite:

Hoh
I am generating an altruistic mind of enlightenment
Within the four immeasurables so that living beings
Who wander up and down the chain of cyclic existence
Because of false images like those cast by the moon in water,
May rest in the sphere of self-knowledge and clear light.

Hoh is an exclamation of amazement. To an ultimate consciousness, all the various external appearances are like the reflection of the moon in water. Just as the reflection appears to be, but is not, a moon, so what appears so vividly real to our conventional consciousness does not truly exist. All phenomena known by our senses – forms, sounds, smells, tastes and tangible objects – are false in that they seem to exist inherently but do not.

The false appearance of objects draws us into error. The force of the attachment of our eye to forms, our ear to sounds, our nose to smells, our tongue to tastes, and our body to feelings draws us back into cyclic existence.

Our lives are like links in a chain, and we wander from one to the other. We are like flies trapped in a jar, circling up and down but remaining in the same situation. We are wanderers, straying through cyclic existences, being born as gods and humans through virtuous actions and as animals, hungry ghosts, or hell-beings through non-virtuous ones. Although we have been wandering in this way from time without beginning, we still have not finished; there seems to be no end. But now that we have met with a profound teaching, we are able to identify ourselves, our own nature, and so can rest in the sphere of self-knowledge and clear light.

It is not sufficient to aspire to this state for yourself alone. You should generate the four immeasurables with the intention that all beings throughout space may rest in this sphere of self-knowledge and clear light.

You should recite the stanza at least six times daily, and practitioners often seek to do so a hundred thousand times. Obstructions in our thoughts and perceptions prevent development; to overcome these obstacles we should fully manifest the altruistic attitude, promising to attain Buddhahood for the sake of others in front of the assembly and asking its members to clear away all obstructions.

At the end of each session, concentrate with great faith on the field of assembly. All present are pleased with your good effort and virtue and bestow blessings in the form of light. You dissolve into that light which then returns to the assembly; they, like a rainbow melting in the sky, dissolve into the central figure, Padmasambhava, and he into his heart, which then melts into space. Consider your mind to be one with the minds of the Buddhas and Bodhisattvas, and stay within meditative equipoise on emptiness as long as you can, without any thoughts or conceptions.

When it is time to leave the session, consider everything that you can see as the illusory creations of a magician. Dedicate the benefit to the welfare of all sentient beings, wishing again that those who have not yet generated a mind of enlightenment might develop it and that those who have already done so may increase it. Using your imagination, reflect on how to dedicate the meritorious power of your session to each and every sentient being throughout space.

With respect to the precepts for developing an altruistic mind of enlightenment, all sentient beings in this great ocean of cyclic existence want happiness but do not know how to cause it; therefore what they want and what they do are at cross-purposes. The goal of this meditation is to generate compassion and love for all these beings.

Take yourself as an example. You seek many kinds of happiness and try to avoid as much suffering as possible. Once you recognize these feelings in yourself, apply this understanding to others. For instance, if you are pricked by a thorn and cannot bear the pain you will say, 'Ouch.' Understand that other beings feel just the same; they do not want suffering any more than you do.

You will then realize that whatever you want is desired by others and that when you struggle to be happy, they do so as well. In this sense you are equal. The more you understand this the more strongly will you think about equality.

When after long meditation you have realized that you and others are equals, the next step is to cherish them more than yourself. Visualize before you someone in great distress. Because virtue creates happiness and its opposite creates suffering, imagine that as you exhale, the power of all your virtues goes out with your breath and enters the distressed being in front of you. Similarly, as you inhale, take all his suffering into yourself, thereby relieving him of it. When you become used to this practice, extend it to others, gradually including more and more, and eventually you will be able to meditate that you are relieving the sufferings of all beings everywhere.

Breathing out your own happiness and breathing in others' suffering is the greatest of all Mahayana paths. Buddha himself generated this altruistic mind of enlightenment through love and compassion while in one of the hot hells. He and another hell-being named Kamarupa were pulling a burning chariot and it occurred to him that instead of the two of them suffering under its heat and weight, it would be better if he bore it alone. He took the flaming harness of the other man and told the guardian, 'I will pull it for both of us.'

The guardian shouted angrily, 'One cannot do it alone, both must pull,' and struck Buddha on the head with a pole.

As he was being hit, Buddha wished, 'May I be able to take on myself the suffering of all the beings in hells.' According to sutra, this was the first time that Buddha generated the altruistic mind of enlightenment. Due to its force he was immediately released from the hell.

In another life Buddha was the son of a man named Dal, whose other male children had died at birth, and because of this bad luck the man called Buddha 'Daughter'. Dal was a merchant who gathered jewels in the ocean, and when Buddha was still a child, his ship sank and he drowned. When the boy grew older, he asked his mother what his father did, so that as was customary he could do the same. His mother was afraid that if she told him, he too would die at sea, so she said, 'Your father dealt in barley.'

Buddha began to trade in barley and soon made a profit, which he brought home to his mother. The other dealers were angry that he had encroached into their field and told him, 'You are not one of us; that was not your father's trade.'

He went to his mother again and asked, 'They say my father did not deal in barley. What did he do?'

'He was an incense trader.' So Buddha began buying and selling incense and soon made four times as much profit as he had done in barley.

The dealers became angry and said, 'You cannot sell incense. That was not your father's business.' Again he inquired about what his father had done, and this time his mother told him he had been a clothier.

Buddha made twice as much money selling cloth as he had done with incense and it was not long before the other clothiers approached him. 'It was not your father's trade to sell cloth; he collected jewels from the ocean. That is your work.'

He went home and informed his mother that he would go to sea to look for jewels as his father had done. She told him then what had become of his father and begged him not to go, but he would not obey her. As he was setting out the next morning, she pleaded with him to stay. He became angry and kicked her in the head. With that, he left and went to sea. Before long his ship broke up in a storm, but he managed to hold onto a plank and drifted ashore on the far side of the ocean.

He had arrived at a very beautiful place called Joy City. Four very good-looking girls took him into their home and fed him extremely well. He was told to eat what he liked and sleep where he chose. Yet after a while, predispositions established by his previous actions forced him to leave. The four girls begged him to stay with them, but he would not listen. They warned him, 'If you must leave us, at least do not go south, or you will have trouble.' He wondered what they could be referring to and headed south.

He soon arrived at an even more marvellous place called Joyous City. There eight girls took care of him and he enjoyed every sort of pleasure imaginable. However it was not long before he told the girls that he was leaving, and no matter how they pleaded, they could not change his mind. Before he left, they told him, 'Whatever you do, do not go south, or you will be in trouble.'

Again he headed south, and came to a still more beautiful city, called Raro. Sixteen girls waited on him and supplied him with every comfort, but before long he left them and continued south despite their many warnings. He sailed on for a long time, occasionally interrupting his travels to stay with an ever-increasing number of beautiful girls, each group more wonderful than the last, satisfying his every wish and never failing to warn him against travelling south.

Eventually he arrived at a nine-storeyed iron house inhabited by horrible red-eyed beings who carried iron whips. He asked one of them, 'What is in this house?' but got no answer. He became very curious about what the house might contain and went inside. It was full of many red-eyed monsters, and seeing them he felt that this must be why he had so often been warned not to go south. He saw on one person's head a revolving wheel that was carving up his brain and churning it into pudding. He approached and asked, 'What did you do to deserve such suffering?'

'I kicked my mother in the head and so have been reborn here. My suffering is very great. What made a fortunate person like you come here?'

The jewel-gatherer's son reflected, 'I too have kicked my mother in the head; this must be an irreversible action the consequences of which I will have to bear.' He began to be afraid and the wheel rose up off the other man's head, moved to his own and started to churn up his brain. At that moment he prayed, 'May this suffering equal that of all other beings who have hit their mothers in the head, and may my undergoing it cause all theirs to disappear.' As soon as he generated this aspiration induced by love and compassion, a voice resounded from the sky, 'He who was bound is freed,' and the wheel rose off his head.

The benefit that comes in meditation from continuously

cultivating the altruistic aspiration to highest enlightenment is vast. Therefore, the Ga-dam-ba Ge-shays took it as the very essence and centre of their practice.

The Ga-dam-ba scholar, Ge-shay Chay-ka-wa (*dGe-bshes 'Chad-kha-ba*) was a master of the Buddhist treatises and highly skilled in the use of words. While visiting another Ge-shay[24] he noticed a small book, opened it and read, 'Take all fault upon yourself. Attribute everything of value to others.' He thought this was a marvellous doctrine and asked where he could find a teacher of this practice. His host answered, 'There is a Ga-dam-ba Ge-shay named Lang-tang-ba (*gLang-thang-pa*) who has a text called *Eight Lines on Training the Mind* which teaches it. Through it one can train in this altruistic attitude.'

Ge-shay Chay-ka-wa felt he must find this teacher who could give him the quintessential instructions on this practice, so when he heard that Lang-tang-ba was in Lhasa, in central Tibet, he set out from his own eastern province to find him. On arrival in Lhasa, he learned that the Ge-shay had died, so he asked who had taken over his old monastery. Hearing that two Ge-shays were disputing about the succession, Ge-shay Chay-ka-wa thought, 'If they are fighting over who should be in charge, then they cannot have the quintessential instructions on training in the altruistic attitude.'

However they actually were not quarrelling like ordinary people.

'You must take charge,' the first one said, 'you are more qualified than I.'

'No I will not,' said the second, 'for you are far more able.'

However Ge-shay Chay-ka-wa did not know this and so he felt that they probably did not have the instruction he was seeking. Thus he went on to another teacher, Sha-ra-ba, who was giving a series of lectures to seven thousand monks. Ge-shay Chay-ka-wa joined the group, but heard nothing about taking all fault upon oneself and attributing everything of value to others. After many days he began to think that this teacher did not have what he sought, but when he met the lama circumambulating a temple, he begged him to sit down so that they might talk for a few minutes. 'What do you want to ask?' said the teacher. 'I have already explained everything I know.'

'Please hear my question,' Ge-shay Chay-ka-wa pleaded. 'What is the importance of the doctrine of taking fault on oneself and attributing what is worthwhile to others?'

'No matter what doctrine you assume, you will not be able to attain Buddhahood unless you have done this practice,' the lama answered.

'Do you have the teaching?'

'Yes. It is my chief practice.'

'Please give it to me.'

'Not until you have studied with me for a long time.'

'I will stay as long as necessary,' said the Ge-shay. He began a thorough study of the eight verses and although they are very short, it took him six years to receive the full teaching. He then went into retreat and cultivated the ability to cherish others instead of himself.

Whenever you cherish others in this way, you do not ever think to gain profit for yourself, but take whatever is worthwhile and give it to others. Practise the thought, 'May all the suffering due to ripen in the continuums of other sentient beings take place in my own instead, and may all my own virtues and the happiness arising from them bear fruit not in my continuum but in theirs.' For beginners like ourselves such an attitude is extremely difficult, but if cultivated in meditation, it can grow to full fruition.

Jam-bay-nel-jor-ba (*Byams-pa'i-rnal-'byor-pa*), whose name means 'Yogi of Love', was lecturing in the open when a man nearby threw a rock at a dog. The yogi called out as if in pain and sank down on his cushion. The people in the audience felt he was making a false display of sympathy for the dog. He said, 'Since you do not believe me, look here,' and he showed them a swelling on his back. The great lama had been able to take on himself the pain that the dog would have suffered.

The Hinayana master Dharmarakshita developed great compassion and generated the altruistic aspiration of a Bodhisattva. Coming upon a very sick man one day, he asked the doctor, 'What medicine does he need?'

'The flesh of a living man. Nothing else will cure him,' said the doctor.

In order to help, Dharmarakshita cut flesh from his thigh, but found it was extremely painful because as a follower of Hinayana tenets, he knew nothing about emptiness.

He sent the flesh to the patient and later learned that the man had recovered. 'Then I am satisfied,' said Dharmarakshita. 'I am glad I was able to relieve his suffering.'

His friends wondered at this. 'How can you be glad?' they asked. 'Surely you regret cutting off so much flesh.'

But Dharmarakshita replied, 'I do not, although the pain is still so great that I cannot sleep.'

Shortly after, he slept a little near dawn during which he dreamed that a shining white being appeared to him and praised him for having done this marvellous thing to help another person. The being rubbed a little saliva on the wound which Dharmarakshita, when he awoke, found had been completely healed. Avalokiteshvara had appeared to him in the dream and given a blessed empowerment which cured his leg.

Through his great altruism Dharmarakshita had cleared away his karmic obstructions, and it is said that he spontaneously came to know the teachings of the Mahayana although he had never studied them. In the same way he was able to recite the six books of Nagarjuna which establish emptiness as the final mode of being of all phenomena.

Our own Buddha was once born as King Lotus, who ruled during the time of a great plague. The king consulted his doctors and asked how the plague might be ended. They told him, 'There is a fish called rohita whose flesh we need as medicine, but we do not know what it is like. The plague has affected our minds, and we have grown stupid.'

Early in the morning on an auspicious date the king put on a new robe, went to his palace roof, and made many offerings and prayers to the Buddhas and Bodhisattvas. With pure Mahayana vows he thought, 'May I take rebirth as this rohita fish,' and jumped off the roof.

He was immediately reborn in a nearby river as a rohita, but because nobody knew he was there, no one came to use him. He swam to the surface and called out in a human voice, 'I am a rohita fish. Please take my flesh.' His voice was heard and people came.

They cut off his flesh first from one and then from the other side, during which the first grew back so that all the people in the area were able to receive a portion. They ate it all and this stopped the plague. The remains as if by magic then said, 'I was King Lotus and took rebirth as this fish in order to help you overcome the plague. Please help me now by being as virtuous as you can.'

The people felt, 'Our good king took rebirth like this to help us. Of course, we will help him in return and practise virtue as much as we can.' Through their subsequent activities the whole country became prosperous and happy.

At another time Buddha was reborn as a turtle. A ship carrying five hundred traders was about to sink when a great turtle appeared and said, 'Please climb on my back and I will save you.' He carried all the five hundred safely to shore, but was so tired that he fell asleep on the beach. When he awoke, he found that eighty thousand bugs were eating him. 'If I return to the water now, all these bugs will die. I am only one person and if my flesh can sustain so many other living beings, then I will stay in this dry place and die.'

Later when Buddha appeared as Shakyamuni, these bugs were reborn as the eighty thousand gods who first came to listen to his teaching. In the chronicles of his previous lives, there are stories of five hundred impure and five hundred pure births; during the former he gave his body many times for the sake of other sentient beings.

After generating an aspirational mind of enlightenment, the next step is to develop a practical one. This entails practising the six perfections: giving, ethics, patience, effort, concentration and wisdom.

In general, there are three types of giving: of things, of relief from fear, and of the doctrine. The latter is when a teacher lectures or gives practices to his students. The gift of things is to make presents of money, clothing, food and so on. Relief from fear is given by removing its cause, as in the case of helping bugs out of puddles.

Gift, giver and recipient are the three spheres or factors of giving. It is especially good to give to people who have been ill for a long time, who have come from far away or to your own teacher. The gift should be your own property, not something stolen from another. The best one is an item that you hold to be extremely important and about which you feel miserly. It should be given without any sense of attachment and for the sole purpose of helping others.

Giving is said to be pure when its three spheres are sealed with the stamp of emptiness. If you can understand the giver, gift and recipient as not existing in their own right, you have achieved the perfection of giving. If you are not able to seal or qualify each of these three in this way, then your gift, though virtuous and helpful to yourself and others, is not an example of the *perfection* of giving.

It is said that although followers of Hinayana give generously, it is not called a perfection, for they do not qualify the three factors as not existing in their own right. But do Hinayanists practise the six perfections at all? Although they practise giving, ethics, patience, effort, concentration and wisdom, there is not a single word in their scriptures about these six as perfections. The difference between the giving of a Hinayanist and a genuine Mahayanist is as great as that between sky and earth. For a Mahayanist, the three aspects of giving are thoroughly qualified by emptiness. If you consider these three spheres of agent, object and action with respect to all six perfections and reflect on their dependent-arising, you will develop a little understanding of what it means to engage in these practices knowing that the three factors of each do not exist in their own right.

The Hinayana practice of ethics mainly consists of keeping the 253 vows of a monk. A Mahayanist strives to maintain the vows of a Bodhisattva as well as those of a monk. The former are all concerned with helping other sentient beings and thus are superior to Hinayana ethics. Whereas the motivation of the Hinayana practice of ethics is to escape from cyclic existence, that of a Bodhisattva is concern for the welfare of other sentient beings.

Similarly the way of cultivating patience, the third perfection, is very different in the two vehicles. A Hinayanist does this because he knows that he himself will benefit greatly whereas a Bodhisattva's patience is induced by compassion. He feels that if he responds angrily to one who is angry with him, it will only bring more trouble to the latter, whose anger will grow. Also, because the field to which a Bodhisattva pays attention – all sentient beings – is so vast, his practice has more force.

With respect to wisdom, a Hinayanist seeks to understand only the emptiness of persons, not that of all other phenomena. Thus he does not strive as hard to cultivate the mental factor of special insight as does a Bodhisattva. Instead he mainly develops a factor of meditative stabilization. A Bodhisattva, however, strives to ascertain the emptiness both of persons and of all phenomena in the world systems.

12 *Vajrasattva Meditation*

Our own non-virtue prevents us from achieving vision and realization of the profound meaning of suchness.[25] Vajrasattva meditation and repetition is a means of purifying non-virtues.

Our mind is like a mirror that needs cleaning although its entity is the essentially pure mind-basis-of-all (*ālayavijñāna*). If a mirror is not clean, the images it reflects cannot be seen clearly; similarly, in order to see and realize suchness, the mind must be purified. The best among many skilful means for so doing is Vajrasattva meditation and repetition.

Unless you engage in a purifying practice, your misdeeds will become as vast as the largest mountain. Revelation and dismemberment of non-virtue is extremely important and it can be done very quickly through the Vajrasattva meditation. Sins are indeed horrible but they have the good feature of being purifiable.

What non-virtues are to be purified? You might have taken a vow of individual liberation and then have broken part of it, or even if you have not taken it in your present life, you may have done so and broken it in the past. There are also contradictions and infractions of Bodhisattva vows, as well as sins involved in breaking tantric vows. All these and other misdeeds not involved with vows such as the ten natural non-virtues (see p. 21) are objects to be confessed, to be broken up and destroyed. Just as when the sun emerges from clouds it shines with great force and magnificence, so does the mind freed from sinful predispositions.[26] There is not one of the many non-virtues accumulated in the past that cannot be purified through revealing and confessing it.

One of Buddha's trainees, named Angulimala, killed 999 people and made a necklace taking one finger from each. Yet through great effort and contrition, even he was able to attain the rank of Arhat. A king who killed his own father merely dropped down into a hell for a moment and then rose out of it because of his powerful contrition.[27]

Perhaps you think it would be possible to commit a sin, confess and then repeat it, but this method will never purify non-virtue. In order to be effective, a confession must possess four powers. The first is that of the object or base, which is the being to whom you confess – in this case Vajrasattva. The second power is a strong sense of contrition and dissatisfaction with whatever misdeeds you have done in the past. The third is an aspiration towards restraint, a strong intention to avoid repeating the deeds in the future. The fourth is to apply an antidote to what you have misdone. In general, this can be any virtuous practice; the specific antidote here is Vajrasattva meditation and repetition.

If you are about to start on a particularly difficult journey, you look for a competent guide in whom to place confidence. In this practice he is Vajrasattva. Shantideva says that no matter how dreadfully one has acted, it can be overcome by depending on a guide, just as even a huge mountain of sin can be consumed like a haystack set on fire by a spark.[28] Vajrasattva meditation and repetition has such power.

The first step is to generate a strong sense of contrition for past sins. In order to do this, you must identify non-virtues as such and recognize these as causes of birth in the unfortunate realms. Confession will bless your mental continuum and free you from the fault of hiding misdeeds.

If you behave badly and then through embarrassment or

fear hide the fact from other meditators, the force of what you have done will grow greatly even while you sleep. Therefore it is necessary at once to inform your lama or those with whom you live, 'I have done such and such. I openly confess it.' For example, if you steal from someone and then hide the fact, not only have you robbed one man but the non-virtuous force of your act expands so that you will reap the effect of having robbed many people. If you reveal it, at the most you will only suffer for having robbed one person.

It is also said, 'Without contrition, no amount of confession will help.' Your own past non-virtues should be considered as poison in your body that must be expelled. You should have a strong sense of shame but not a wish to hide. Even fear would be appropriate because by misdeeds you create the causes for rebirth in lower migrations of extreme suffering. You should have a strong sense that what you have done is wrong and make a strong intention not to repeat it.

In order to carry out your intention to refrain from non-virtue in the future, you need mindfulness and introspection that are able to catch even slight tendencies towards non-virtue. Coupled with watchfulness there must be a very strong and urgent resolution not to repeat the mistake even if it should cost your life. Without a strong sense of restraint it is not possible to purify sins.

Once you have visualized the special object, Vajrasattva, generated contrition and created an aspiration to refrain from such acts in the future, you are ready to apply the antidote. Bowing down to the Buddhas and Bodhisattvas, taking delight in the virtues of others, and dedicating all your virtue to highest enlightenment will counter previous non-virtue. Generating an aspirational and practical mind of enlightenment together with sustaining the entity of emptiness in meditative equipoise are also strong antidotes.

A very simple fellow who was a student of Gam-bo-ba had traded briskly in religious texts, images and other religious objects. He went to Gam-bo-ba and asked how to purify this sin. He was told, 'You must earn again as much profit as you have made in this way and use it to build a temple.'

He worked hard to establish a temple complete with beautiful images and other works of art, but the task soon became troublesome because it left him no time to meditate.

So he returned to Lama Gam-bo-ba and said, 'I am spending so much time acquiring images and books for the temple that I am distracted and can find no opportunity to meditate.'

His lama told him, 'If you can sustain an understanding of suchness for even a moment, this will purify a whole mountain of non-virtue.' This special means of purifying sins depends on realizing the empty entity of the mind. Coupling this with Vajrasattva meditation and repetition is particularly powerful.

Sit in the adamantine cross-legged posture and visualize the seat of Vajrasattva an arrow length above your head. You should not see yourself as a deity at this time, so the seat is above your normal head. It is a white cushion in the form of a lotus with 100,000 petals, the stem of which descends through the top of your head to a depth of four finger-widths. On top of the lotus is a full-moon disc, and above that the letter *hūṃ* in white. Suddenly the *hūṃ* turns into Vajrasattva, who is your own lama appearing in that form. Seated in the adamantine cross-legged posture, his body is pure white, bright as a snow mountain reflecting the light of a hundred thousand suns; he has one head and two hands, the right holding a vajra and the left a bell.

He has a Complete Enjoyment Body and thus is graced with thirteen jewelled adornments and five of cloth. The jewelled ones are a crown, earrings, garland, necklace, bracelets above the elbows, knee rings, anklets and sandals. The cloth adornments are a headdress, shawl, loose upper garment, belt and lower garment wrapped round the legs. He sits embracing his consort, Great Dignity.

His body is like a rainbow shining in space or an image in a mirror. It appears, yet is empty of obstructiveness. Meditate on his form until even the whites of his eyes and dark pupils are sharp and clear. Do not think that his body is a coarse one made of silver, white stone or any similar substance. It is made of light. Do not imagine him as a flat painting but in three dimensions, vivid down to the finest detail. He is clear and diaphanous throughout.

You should be very ashamed of past errors and be determined to reveal them to Vajrasattva. Make a petition to him, 'I will cleanse all the sinful deeds that I have done since beginningless cyclic existence. I will purify the ten non-virtues that I have done since time without beginning. I will cleanse the five heinous acts that I have accumulated. In the past I have broken the vows of individual liberation, those of Bodhisattvas, and the tantric ones. Please cleanse all of these. I have lied and broken many oaths; please purify them.'

Next, commit yourself to refrain from non-virtuous accumulations in the future. Fully absorbed in these intentions, recite:

Āḥ
Above the crown of my own normal head
Are cushions of a white lotus and a moon.
From the *hūṃ* in their centre Vajrasattva appears
With the clear white body of Complete Enjoyment,
Holding vajra and bell and embracing his consort.

I ask you for refuge and to cleanse my sins, confessed
With a strong mind of contrition. Henceforth
I will refrain from them though it cost my life.
On your heart's broad moon is the letter *hūṃ*
Surrounded by the mantra. Through repeating
This mantra your continuum is stirred, and from the place
Of union of the father and mother's blissful sport
Comes the cloud of the nectar of the mind of enlightenment,
Falling like drops of camphor. Through it may all polluted
Actions and afflictions which cause all suffering,

Sickness, spirits, sins, obstructions, faults, infractions,
And defilements of myself and all beings
In the three realms be made completely clean.

The initial syllable, *Āḥ*, symbolizes non-produced suchness. Between Vajrasattva and his consort at heart level is a
flat moon disc with a white letter *hūṃ* upright in its centre.
Standing on the outer edge of the moon disc are the letters
of the 100-syllable mantra. These letters are white, small
and fine as if they were written with white hairs. They are
cold, and your repetition causes them to melt like ice so that
white nectar flows down between Vajrasattva and his
consort Great Dignity through their place of union onto the
lotus and into the stem. Passing down the stem, it flows into
your own head and body.

When you become skilled at visualizing Vajrasattva
above your head, imagine other sentient beings meditating
with him on their heads. Slowly increase the number of
beings until you are able to imagine as many as there are
particles of earth. All of them are engaged in the Vajrasattva
meditation with you. Recite with great faith and energy the
mantra:

*Oṃ Vajrasattva, samayam anupālaya, Vajrasattva, tvenopatiṣṇṭha,
dṛḍho me bhava, sutoṣnyo me bhava, supoṣnyo me bhava, anurakto
me bhava, sarva-siddhiṃ me prayachchha, sarva-karmasu cha me
chittaṃ shrīyaṃ kuru, hūṃ ha ha ha ha hoḥ, Bhagavan-sarva-
tathāgata-vajra, mā me muñcha, vajrī bhava, mahāsamaya-sattva, āḥ
hūṃ (Oṃ* Vajrasattva, keep [your] pledge.[29] Vajrasattva, reside
[in me]. Make me firm. Make me satisfied. Fulfil me. Make me
compassionate. Grant me all siddhis. Also, make my mind
virtuous in all actions. *Hūṃ ha ha ha ha hoḥ* all the blessed
Tathagatas, do not abandon me, make me indivisible. Great
Pledge Being, *āḥ hūṃ.*)

oṃ: the appearance in letter form of the indestructible vajra
body essence of all Sugatas. It is an expression of one's
intention and of luck.
vajra: the nature of the wisdom of emptiness, indestructible
by whatsoever cause.

sattva: the method, great compassion.

Vajrasattva: the great bliss which has in equal taste emptiness and great compassion, indivisibly in union. In a state of defiled impurity it is cyclic existence; in a state of diminishing impurity brought about by the states of purification it is the path, and in a state of total separation from defilement it is Buddhahood. The word is in the vocative case; thus he [the manifestation of the above as a person] is being called by name in order to beseech his consideration.

samayam: pledges, meaning those which one will not pass beyond (accusative, as the object of 'keep').

anupālaya: keep, meaning to keep his pledge with respect to me (imperative).

tvena: by you, Vajrasattva.

upatiṣṇṭha: reside (imperative). Vajrasattva is being called upon to reside in oneself.

dṛḍho: firm (nominative), referring to the manner in which Vajrasattva resides in oneself.

me: me (dative). Though the Vajrasattva which is the mode of subsistence [of all phenomena] pervades and resides in everything from the start – self and other, cyclic existence and nirvana, the stable and the moving – Vajrasattva [is being asked to] reside in oneself in a manifest manner in the sense of one's own self-knowledge of what has hitherto [only] been identified.

bhava: be (imperative), having the sense of 'make.'

sutoṣnyo: well-satisfied, very satisfied.

me: me (dative).

bhava: be (imperative), having the sense of 'make.' One is beseeching Vajrasattva to make oneself very satisfied through tasting the joy of freedom from conceptual elaborations and the great bliss.

supoṣnyo: very or well increased. With *me bhava* as before, the meaning is, 'Increase the wisdom of non-dual bliss and emptiness in me.'

anurakto: pleased. With *me bhava* as before, the meaning is, 'Make me compassionate,' in the sense of 'Make me loving

through the great compassion of the state of union in which
the defilements of attachment are abandoned afar.'

sarva: all.

siddhiṃ: feat[s] (accusative).

me: me (dative).

prayachchha: grant, bestow (imperative). 'Grant me all
feats,' great and small, supreme and common.

sarva: all.

karmasu: actions (locative).

cha: and, also.

me: me (genitive).

chittaṃ: mind (accusative).

shrīyaṃ: virtue (accusative).

kuru: make (imperative). 'Make my mind virtuous in all
actions.' Since the mind precedes all actions, if the mind is
virtuous, all actions are virtuous; hence, one is urging
Vajrasattva to make one's mind virtuous. One is beseeching
Vajrasattva for the realization of the ultimate secret that the
many creations of appearances – cyclic existence and
nirvana – are emanated from the self-force of the one vajra,
the great bliss consciousness, and that no matter how much
is emanated, they do not pass beyond the nature of the mind
itself – great bliss.

hūṃ: the seed [syllable] of Vajrasattva sealing the five
Tathagata lineages – the pure nature of the five aggregates
and so forth.

ha ha ha ha: the pure nature of the four joys.

hoḥ: the pure nature of objects – forms, sounds, odours,
tastes, tangible objects, and mental objects – and subjects –
eye, ear, nose, tongue, body and mental consciousnesses.

bhagavan: Blessed One, so called because of possessing
either the four conquests or the six fortunes.

sarva: all.

tathāgata: one who has passed to the limit of reality just as
it is.

vajra: non-dual wisdom. The nominative case is affixed
with a vocative meaning since one is asking for the

consideration of all Tathagatas.

mā: not.

me: me.

muñcha: abandon (imperative). 'Do not abandon me,' meaning, 'Do not allow the great bliss wisdom realizing suchness to become separated from me,' or, 'Through the bonds of boundless great compassion never let me loose.'

vajrī: having a vajra. With *bhava*, 'Make me vajric.' It indicates the manner of non-abandonment by Vajrasattva.

mahā: great.

samaya: pledge.

sattva: being, hero (vocative).

āḥ: the indestructible letter which is the essence of the speech-vajra of all Tathagatas. One is beseeching the Great Pledge Being, Vajrasattva, to establish oneself in the entity of the great wisdom in which all Tathagatas without exception are equal.

If possible, repeat the mantra twenty-one times each day so as to maintain continuous purification.

As the nectar enters you, it cleanses you from all contaminated actions of the past and the afflictions of desire, hatred and ignorance which are the causes of suffering. As a result, all sicknesses are excreted through the lower parts of the body as pus and foul blood. Many black and rotten substances emerge – dirt, dust, ink and evil spirits in the form of frogs, toads, spiders, scorpions, snakes and tadpoles.

The nectar enters through your head and washes these forms out through the lower part of the body – the anal and genital openings and the soles of your feet. As they begin to flow out, the earth opens to a depth of nine storeys. All the messengers and workers of the lords of death – people whose karmic relationship with you is such that they would cause your life to be shortened – are there, together with all those to whom you have any obligation. For example, in our beginningless continuum of lives we have eaten a great quantity of meat, and the animals whose flesh was used now come to reclaim their loan. Anyone who has lent us money or goods is also to be repaid at this time. They stand with hands and mouths open upwards. The ugly forms that have descended from your body are transformed into whatever these beings need and want – money, clothes, food, drink, or anything else they may desire. Satisfied and content, they return from whence they came and the earth closes again. In this way you are able to clear all your debts.

Your body is so purified that it becomes clear inside and out, like crystal. Like milk pouring into a crystal vessel, the nectar from Vajrasattva and his consort fills your body from bottom to top.

It is excellent to imagine all these processes simultaneously, but beginners usually take them one at a time until they can keep the whole process in mind. To repeat: the first step is to focus your attention on the white *hūṃ* standing on the lotus, then on the clear forms of Vajrasattva and his consort and the letters melting between their hearts. Next, concentrate on the falling nectar and visualize all the foul entities flowing from your body. Visualize all male and female beings to whom you are in any way indebted and imagine their receiving your beautiful gifts and being delighted with them. Imagine that you are repaying these beings for everything they have given you in any form over hundreds of past lifetimes. Imagine that your own body becomes clear and diaphanous, with the energy centres at the base of the spine, navel, heart, throat and head filled with brilliant white nectar.

As the nectar arrives at your crown centre, you attain joy and the vessel initiation eliminating obstructions due to non-virtuous actions. When it reaches your neck centre, you win supreme joy and the secret initiation eliminating the obstructions preventing liberation. When it fills your heart centre, you achieve special joy and the wisdom initiation eliminating the obstructions to omniscience. When it arrives at the navel centre, you attain innate joy and the word initiation eliminating obstructions in the form of predispositions established by former deeds.

Until this point in the visualization you have been reciting the hundred-syllable mantra. Now stop and consider that as an effect of these abandonments and attainments, you have attained the Four Bodies of a Buddha. These are the ultimate goals of the Mahayana. Remain in meditative equipoise in this state as long as possible, and then recite:

O protector, through ignorance I have
Contradicted and broken my pledges.
May I be guarded by the lama protector!
I take refuge in the leader of living beings,
The leader holding a vajra
Whose nature is great compassion.
I earnestly confess all pollution of my pledges of body,
Speech and mind – fundamental and secondary. Please
Cleanse and purify all my masses of defilement – sins,
Obstructions, faults, and infractions.

This is an earnest confession of all past non-virtues, from killing through to wrong views as well as the five heinous deeds. Vajrasattva is compassionate, and you are looking to him for refuge and help. He smiles and laughs with great delight in your virtue and answers:

O child of good lineage, all your sins, obstructions,
Faults and infractions are purified.

As soon as he finishes speaking, Vajrasattva and his consort melt into light – like ice into water – and dissolve into you, as does the lotus. Then, you instantaneously become Vajrasattva with the consort Great Dignity seated on your lap.

This is not a body of flesh and bone; it is like a rainbow in the sky, appearing yet empty. Consider that you have the complete form, ornaments, posture and consort that you previously visualized as Vajrasattva. At your heart is a tiny moon disc, the size of a flat mustard seed. In its centre is a blue letter *hūṃ*, and in front of the *hūṃ* is a white letter *oṃ*, to the right are the yellow letters *vajra*, behind is a red *sa*, and to the left a green *ttva*. Each of these letters emanates inconceivable rays of light in its own colour shining in all directions.

At the end of each ray are the five goddesses who offer visible forms, sounds, odours, tastes and tangible objects to the Buddhas and Bodhisattvas of the ten directions – north, south, east, west, the four intermediate directions, above and below. The goddesses offer everything of value to the Buddhas and Bodhisattvas, each dissolving with her offering into the seat of the sense consciousness where the gift is experienced – eye, ear, nose, tongue or body. Through these magnificent offerings your accumulation of meritorious power becomes complete and the last obstructions are cleared away. The dissolving of the goddesses and their gifts generates an inconceivable bliss in the minds of the Buddhas and Bodhisattvas, causing them to emit white rays of light, endowing you with all common, uncommon and special siddhis. Consider that you have become fully enlightened with the Four Bodies of a Buddha. This meditation is a future dependent-arising, leading to your eventual transformation into an actual Buddha.

Rays of light from the letters at your heart radiate once more and descend to the hells like a great rain. The rays are like wish-granting jewels bestowing whatever the hell-beings want – freedom from heat, cold and so forth.

Like a sun shining in a dark place, the rays clear away all darkness and suffering, spreading first to the hells and then to the realms of hungry ghosts, animals, humans, demigods and gods. The realms of all six types of living beings are purified and transformed into the eastern pure lands of Vajrasattva, called the Very Joyous. All beings in all world systems are transformed into the five Vajrasattvas: white, yellow, red, green and blue.

Throughout the visualization, recite, *Oṃ Vajrasattva hūṃ*. This practice, known as the eradication of cyclic existence, establishes the future dependent-arising of your ability to eliminate the misery of all sentient beings throughout space and bring about their welfare. Maintain the meditation and repetition for as long as you can.

When concluding the session, imagine that all pure lands and Vajrasattvas throughout space melt into light and dissolve into you. Your own body dissolves into the white letter *oṃ* at your heart, the *oṃ* into the yellow letters *vajra*, the *vajra* into the red letter *sa*, the *sa* into the green letters *ttva*, the *ttva* into the *u* of *hūṃ*; this into the long vowel sign which slowly dissolves into the lower part of the letter *ha*, then in turn into the top line, the drop, and the symbol called *nāḍa*, which disappears like a rainbow vanishing in space.

Set yourself in meditative equipoise; let your mind remain fused with this space-like void for as long as you can. When thoughts and conceptions begin to arise, do not be overwhelmed by them but imagine that Vajrasattva's own pure land has suddenly and adventitiously arisen out of clear space. Before leaving your meditation cushion, dedicate the merit of the session to the welfare of all sentient beings throughout space and repeat the mantra once more. If suitable, continue saying it to yourself as you go about your daily activities. Leave your session with the thought that all sentient beings have become Vajrasattvas, and with a small part of your mind retain the thought that you are in a pure land. Consider all appearances as the illusions of a magician.

13 Offering Mandala

Great meritorious power is required for developing an understanding of suchness, and mandalas are offered as a means of generating this power.[30] There are two collections of power: merit and wisdom, the former being conceivable, while the latter is not. Through completing that of merit, the Form Bodies of a Buddha are attained, and through that of wisdom, the Truth Bodies.

Attainment of Buddhahood means endowment with the Two Bodies and to do this you must have their two causes, the collections of merit and wisdom. Because we do not have sufficient merit, we are unable to cognize emptiness; without understanding this there is no possibility of attaining Buddhahood. The generation of a special innate wisdom that directly cognizes emptiness is an imprint or result of having amassed the two collections of merit and wisdom and relied on the quintessential instructions of a lama.

Even when you have accumulated sufficient meritorious power to cognize emptiness, you still have to complete the collection of merit. As Tilopa said to Naropa, 'Do not cease amassing the collections until you have thoroughly understood the empty nature of dependently arisen appearances.'

Tantra has the special practice of making offerings to millions of Buddha Lands as a technique for completing the collections of virtuous power, which would be impossible if it depended entirely on physical offerings. With imagination, however, one can make inconceivable offerings to a great many Buddha Lands simultaneously. As much as you are able to imagine, so much meritorious power are you able to accumulate.

Two mandalas are involved in this practice, one which you offer and another in front of you representing the Buddhas, Bodhisattvas and deities to whom you make the offering. If you are wealthy, use gold and silver as the base of your mandala, or one of secondary quality made out of bronze or other metal, but if you are poor, a smooth stone will serve equally well.

Many substances can be offered on the mandala – jewels, medicinal fruits and so forth. The humblest offering is grain, such as rice, barley, or wheat, with which you can mix a few precious stones or coins if you have any. A yogi who has nothing, not even rice, would use grains of sand. It is best to change the rice or grains daily, offering it to birds and other animals and giving the coins to the poor. If this is not possible, the rice can be changed weekly or as often as you can afford.

Take the rimmed base of the mandala and rub it clean with your hand. Holding it in your left hand, pick up a handful of rice and place it in the centre. This heap represents Vairochana surrounded by his retinue of many deities of the Buddha lineage. Place a second heap in front of the first to represent Akshobhya and his retinue of deities in the vajra lineage. Each grain of rice serves as a base of imagination of one of these beings. To the right of Vairochana place a third pile of rice representing Ratnasambhava surrounded by deities of the jewel lineage, a fourth behind Vairochana to symbolize Amitabha and his retinue of the lotus lineage, and a fifth on Vairochana's left to represent Amoghasiddhi with his retinue of the karma lineage.

Set this recipient mandala in front of you as the field of assembly to which you will offer the mandala of offering. It is also helpful to have an image to serve as a basis for imagination, but in any case you should imagine the Buddhas of the five lineages and their retinues. You may also arrange various other offerings before you – perfumed water, incense, flowers and so forth.

Take a few grains of rice in your left hand and with it grasp the circular base of the offering mandala. The grains signify flowers and the base represents the gold base of the thousand million world systems. Rub the surface of the base with your wrist and forearm in a circular clockwise motion while reciting the seven-branched prayer:

Hrīḥ

I bow down with emanations of my body
As many as the particles of the lands.

I offer through the power of meditation all appearances
Actually arranged or imagined as Seals of offering.

Within the Truth Bodies of clear light I confess
All non-virtuous actions done through the three doors.

I admire all collections of virtue
That are included within the two truths.

I request the wheels of teaching of the three vehicles
To be turned for the trainees of the three lineages.

I pray you to remain without passing away
Until cyclic existence is emptied [of all beings].

I dedicate as causes of the great enlightenment
All virtuous roots amassed in the past, present and future.

The purpose in cleaning the surface of the mandala is not to remove external dirt but to clear away defilements in your own mental continuum. Some Ga-dam-bas offered so many mandalas and cleaned them so well that their wrists and arms developed sores; they then changed the angle of their arm a little, and again when new sores appeared. It might seem an unnecessary hardship to use your arm when a cloth would do better, but that is not the point. The goal is to clear away your own obstructions; therefore it is important to use your own body, imagining all the while that with the wisdom of selflessness you are purifying the mandala of non-produced reality of the stains of ignorance.

Next, while still holding the rim in your left hand, recite, '*Oṃ vajra bhūmi āḥ hūṃ*' (*Oṃ* vajra base *āḥ hūṃ*). This refers to the circular plate held in your hand which symbolizes the gold base of the world system. Dip the thumb and ring fingers of your right hand into perfumed water and sprinkle it around the rim of the mandala to symbolize washing the world base. Then take several grains of rice and sprinkle them clockwise around the rim, imagining that you are setting up a mountain range. Place a handful of rice in the centre; this is the basis of the system rimmed by mountains with Mount Meru at its axis. With handfuls of rice set up the eastern continent in front and the southern, western and northern continents to the right, back and left of Mount Meru. Then take the mandala base in both hands and imagine you hold all the great pleasures and delights that anyone in all the world systems could possibly desire. Offer this universe of delightful offerings to the field of assembly, imagining that all actions and predispositions capable of causing rebirth as a hungry ghost are cleared away for yourself and all beings throughout space.

Each time you make the offering, pour the mandala out towards the Buddhas and Bodhisattvas represented by the other mandala in front of you, except for the last time, when you should pour it towards yourself. This symbolizes their bestowal on you of all siddhis in return for the mandala offering you have made. The seven branches need be recited only once at the beginning of each session.

First, offer the thousand million world systems filled with precious substances and the wealth of gods and humans together with your own body to the Emanation Body in order to attain that Body yourself. Offer the land of an Enjoyment Body so that you may come to use that land which is a heavily adorned highest pure land of great bliss.

Finally, offer the Truth Body so that you yourself may come to use the land of that Body. Imagine these offerings vividly while reciting:

Oṃ āḥ hūṃ

Through offering in full the lands of a thousand million world systems

Each having a thousand million worlds, filled with the seven precious substances

And wealth of gods and humans, as well as my body and resources,

May I attain the reign of a universal monarch of doctrine.

Through offering a heavily adorned highest pure land of great bliss

With the five definite attributes and groups of the five lineages

And inconceivable cloud masses of desirable offerings,

May I come to make use of the pure land of an Enjoyment Body.

Through offering pure appearances and beings, the encased youthful body,

The adornment of sport in reality with unimpeded compassion,

A land purified of apprehension of body and drops,[31]

May I come to make use of the land of a Body of Truth.

'*Oṃ āḥ hūṃ*' is recited to purify the land basis. Think that by reciting the syllable *oṃ*, all beings and environments of the entire world system are purified. Through the force of reciting *āḥ*, everything in the universe is transformed into a pleasant object suitable to be offered to Buddhas and Bodhisattvas. When *hūṃ* is recited, the very substance of the world turns into as many offerings as you are capable of imagining.

Every world within a world system has four continents, one each in the east, south, west and north; our own habitation is the southern continent. Between each of these continents are two smaller islands. At the centre of each world system is a great Mount Meru, containing the cities of the demi-gods. Gods of the desire realm also live there in pure lands, and the heavens of the four Great Royal Lineages stand at peaks in each of the four directions. In the space above the mountain lie the Joyous Heaven (*Tuṣhita*) and the higher lands.

A single Mount Meru with its four major continents and eight subcontinents is called a world, and there are one thousand million such worlds in a world system. Here a thousand million of these systems is being offered.

When offering a mandala to Buddhas and Bodhisattvas, imagine that you hold all these thousand million world systems containing a thousand million worlds filled by precious substances – gold, silver, turquoise and so forth. The marvellous resources of gods and humans as well as your own body and resources are offered to the Emanation Body.

The Enjoyment Body resides in an eastern pure land called the Heavily Adorned and known as the Highest Pure Land because it lies above all worldly lands. It is also called the Highest Pure Land of Great Bliss because none of the sufferings found in our world exist there; everything is pleasant and conducive to practice.

The five Buddha lineages to whom these offerings are made are Akshobhya in the east, Ratnasambhava in the south, Amitabha in the west, Amoghasiddhi in the north, and Vairochana in the centre. The offerings are described as inconceivable, not because they are beyond the mind but because they are created or emanated by a mind that is inconceivable to the ordinary intellect, and their numbers are too vast to be counted as one, two and so on. 'Appearances' refers to the external environment; 'beings' means the persons within that environment seen in their pure form as tenth-ground Bodhisattvas in the retinue of an Enjoyment Body.

The entity to be purified in oneself is the encased youthful body which is described to beginners as the Tathagata nature or Buddha nature found in each and every sentient being. Its nature is immutable. When our adventitious defilements are abandoned, we understand that a Buddha has been there primordially. The youthful body that is presently encased by our own predispositions will eventually have all the activities of a Buddha endowed with unimpeded compassion. The youthful body is not at all similar to the conceivable or apprehendable phenomena to which we are accustomed, but is sealed or qualified by the view of emptiness. In order to free this youthful body from its encasement in our own ignorance and predispositions, we must purify our apprehension of the channels, winds [that is, energies] and drops of refined essence in our body. In this way it is possible to develop a view purified of all apprehensions of visionary bodies and drops of light. This purity, which is like a Truth Body, is then offered to the actual Truth Body. In this offering there is neither subject nor object, for both have been transcended.

It is sometimes said that if holding the plate becomes too difficult, the whole offering can be done through imagination alone, but my root lama told me that this is not permissible. No matter how much your arm aches, it is necessary to retain the plate in your hand as a means of removing your obstructions.

At the end of the session slow down your recitation and set the offering mandala on the altar. A great light then pours forth from the five Buddha lineages and spreads through all world systems purifying all sentient beings. Like water being poured into water, all beings throughout space dissolve into every part of your body. Imagine that the five Buddha lineages emit rays of light that enter and endow you with the Buddhas' own mind and realization. After imagining that you have become equal to them, let your own body dissolve into space. Remain in this state of the space-like meditative equipoise of a Truth Body as long as you are able.

14 Cutting Attachment

Many adepts and yogis in India and Tibet have no possessions to use as offerings.[32] They are beggars without any material means of amassing the collections of merit, so they accumulate merit by offering their own bodies. Cutting attachment is a beggar's means of amassing merit and is of such great value that it is included in the internal preparations even though it is not preparatory but part of the actual session.

Cutting attachment here is a form of offering, in this case of one's own body, which one cherishes above everything. Because this giving involves the most cherished possession, the benefit is much greater than in other forms of charity.

From beginningless time we have been far too fond of our bodies. Such self-cherishing is a great mistake and causes much suffering. Offering the body helps to overcome this misconception. If you are skilled in visualization, imagine a drop of light in the central channel just above the navel centre. The drop is supported by wind [energy] and the fierce black goddess stands on top of it. She holds a curved knife in her right hand, a skull in her left and near her right ear is the head of a pig. Send your consciousness, fused with her, out into space through the Brahma opening at the crown of your head. Emitted in this form, your consciousness passes into the actual black goddess visualized above your head. Then recite:

Phaṭ

No longer cherishing the body, the god demon [of distraction]
    is overcome.
The mind emerges into the expanse of space through the
    Brahma opening
Overcoming the death-lord demon and turning into the fierce
    goddess.
Her left hand holds a skull as an instrument and her right
A curved knife conquering the demon of afflictions, cutting off
The skull and overcoming the demon of the form aggregate.
She sets it on a hearth of human skulls which form the Three
    Bodies.
Inside it the corpse filling the thousand million worlds is
    distilled
Into pure nectar by the syllables, *a* and *haṃ*,
And is purified, increased and transformed
By the power of the three syllables.

Repeat for as long as seems appropriate; '*Oṃ āḥ hūṃ.*'

The word '*Phaṭ*' is a symbol of method and wisdom. As
you say it, imagine that your consciousness in the form of
the fierce goddess rises up the central channel. It emerges
through the Brahma opening and becomes undifferentiable
from the goddess herself. Through forsaking your usual
cherishing of the body, the god demon of distraction is
overcome. This god demon is so called because gods are too
happy and thus are distracted from practice. Because your
consciousness has left your body, think that you have
overcome the Lord of Death.

As soon as your consciousness enters the body of the
goddess, imagine that your former body is now a corpse
which slumps to the ground. No longer of normal size, it is
as large as Mount Meru, and you, who are now the goddess,
use the curved knife in your right hand to cut off the skull
just above the eyebrows. The knife symbolizes the fierce
black goddess's complete victory over the demons of desire,
hatred and ignorance. Feel that you are able to overcome the
root of afflictions, for in cutting off the skull you defeat the

demon of the form aggregate to which there is such great attachment. The skull is now so large that it can hold the entire body, equal in size to all the thousand million worlds of the entire world system.

After the goddess cuts off the skull, three human skulls the size of mountains magically appear in front of her as a hearth. These skulls symbolize the Three Bodies. She sets your former skull on the hearth formed by these skulls, at which point it expands until she can place the rest of your body inside it.

Huge clouds gather over the hearth. Beneath it is a red letter *a* ready to burst into flame. Your own strong faith causes it to blaze up, heating the skull and everything inside it. The huge ice-like corpse melts and begins to boil. As the bubbles rise to the top of the skull cauldron, all the dirt and scum of the body spill over, leaving pure nectar. The steam rises and melts a cold white *haṃ* which stands upside down above the skull. Melting like a snow mountain, it drips down into the skull, mixing with and increasing the pure essence distilled from the corpse.

The force of the sound, '*Oṃ āḥ hūṃ,*' recited by you as Vajrayogini, transforms, purifies and increases this essence. The syllable *oṃ* purifies the contents, cleaning away all defilement; the *āḥ* increases it to the point where, like a great ocean, it could never be consumed, and the *hūṃ* transforms the nectar into whatever sentient beings desire. Imagine vividly this purification process while reciting, '*Oṃ āḥ hūṃ.*'

Think that your own lama, accompanied by all the accomplished yogis and adepts from Shakyamuni until the present, has appeared in front of you on marvellous cushions. They are surrounded by protectors of doctrine who hold skulls, knives and ritual daggers. The protectors in turn are encircled by all beings who are hostile to you or to whom you owe a debt of any kind. They are your guests and you will offer them the pure nectar in the skull as drink.

The Buddhas, lamas, personal deities, yogis and

Bodhisattvas do not have tongues as we do; theirs are in the shape of a flat half-vajra, and they take your offering by using a ray of light as a straw to draw the pure substance into themselves. The nectar never decreases, for your mantra recitation continually renews the supply. As the high guests partake of your offering, think that you have completed the collections of merit and wisdom and consider that all sins, obstructions, non-virtues and so forth that you have accumulated since beginningless time are purified. All infractions of vows and pledges are cleansed and you acquire the common and superior siddhis. The high guests are pleased with your offering and bestow on you the four initiations.

Next the protectors draw up the nectar using their own hand symbols – wheel, vajra, and so forth – as straws. They also are extremely satisfied with your offering. Once again, think that you have attained the common and superior siddhis and that all obstructions are purified. Dwell in the thought that the protectors of doctrine are removing all obstacles to your own ability to explain and teach doctrine. This is the first allotment to the high guests, through which all their intentions, hopes and aspirations are fulfilled.

Next, make the allotment to the other guests, the sentient beings gathered before you. If you are skilled in imagination, visualize as many white, yellow, red, green and blue fierce goddesses as there are sentient beings in the world systems. Each goddess holds a skull in her left hand which she dips into the larger skull and fills with nectar. She then offers this marvellous drink to the six types of beings – denizens of hells, hungry ghosts, animals, humans, demi-gods and gods – to whom you owe any debt. Think that the recipients are wholly satisfied by your offering.

Sentient beings are numberless and if it is difficult to visualize so many fierce goddesses, you can imagine one who dips her skull into the larger one and sprinkles nectar to all beings throughout space. Those who want clothing receive it, those desiring wealth become rich, those wishing for a husband, wife, son or daughter receive it. As all are utterly satisfied in terms of their own wishes, think that all your debts to them have been repaid.

When you have completed the first allotment to the low guests, the boiling nectar is stirred by huge waves. Imagine that great clouds of offering, held aloft by broad beams of light and huge rainbows, rise through the steam. On the clouds are umbrellas, banners, white conch shells and anything else suitable for offering. Through offering these to the high field of Buddhas and so forth, all difficulties that stand in the way of achieving enlightenment are pacified and you once more imagine that you have completed all the collections of merit. In return for your offering, the high guests bestow upon you the common and superior siddhis.

The ocean of nectar is stirred again and a light rain falls upon the sentient beings gathered round you, granting their wishes. Groups of goddesses are generated from the streaming rays of light, bestowing further offerings on the lower guests of cyclic existence. Those beings too shy to come forward and receive gifts are touched in the distance by the rays of light and obtain their heart's desire. All infirmities such as blindness or lameness are fully healed, even for those far away. Each male is transformed into an Avalokiteshvara, and each female into a Tara.

Recite '*oṃ āḥ hūṃ*,' continuously throughout the visualization, and when the offerings are complete, say:

Phaṭ
Offerings are made to the high guests and their intentions are
    fulfilled.
Masses of merit completed, I attain the common and supreme
    siddhis.
The low guests of cyclic existence are pleased and all my debts
    are cleared.
Especially all those who harm and obstruct are well satisfied,
Sicknesses, spirits, and interruptors vanish in the expanse,
Bad circumstance and selfishness are all reduced to dust.
At last all that is left of the offerings and recipients
Is the unfabricated *a* in the Great Perfection nature.

Since beginningless time we have killed beings, eaten their flesh and borrowed or robbed them of their wealth. All these debts have now been paid, so that all spirits or beings who may have wished to harm you are thoroughly pacified and all conditions conflicting with an understanding of emptiness are purified. The conception of an inherently existent person, which you have had since time without beginning, is destroyed and reduced to dust. Finally all the voluminous offerings and the multitude of recipients are transformed into the unfabricated emptiness, the Great Perfection nature, the unfabricated *a* – symbol of uncreated reality.

Early in the night, when the sky has just turned black and the moon and stars have not yet appeared, is the best time for practising the stages of visualization in cutting attachment because that is when spirits roam about to find flesh and blood for food. Your offering so satisfies them that they do not have to harm other beings to nourish themselves.

The basic books on cutting attachment come from the Bodhisattva Tara, and its source is the teaching of emptiness in the *Perfection of Wisdom Sutras* which were brought from Naga-land by Nagarjuna.

Though exorcism usually means to banish a spirit from someone else, here it may be taken to mean driving egoism out of oneself. The practice in Tibet originated with Bodhidharma,[18] who received the transmission from Aryadeva in India and taught what is now called the male system of cutting attachment. He visited Tibet five times, and in the fifth taught cutting attachment to a female disciple, Ma-ji-lap-drön (*Ma-gcig-lab-sgron*), who became a very great adept and eventually originated a female variant of the practice. As a rule, Tibetans went to India to learn Buddhism, but Ma-ji-lap-drön was an exception in that many Indians came to Tibet to learn the female form of cutting attachment from her, and it became the only practice to spread from Tibet to India.

15 Guru Yoga

The sixth of the special internal preparations, guru yoga, is the supreme method of generating the ultimate cognition.[33] It is a means of entering the state of blessed empowerment.

To prepare the mind for this practice, imagine your own highly endowed lama before you in space and develop a strong wish to achieve whatever he teaches. Unless you have faith in him and a sense of his pure appearance, the ultimate cannot be cognized. When you have generated these, you are ready to begin guru yoga, which consists of visualizing the field of assembly, performing the seven-branched service, and making an earnest supplication.

VISUALIZING THE FIELD OF ASSEMBLY

It is difficult for people like ourselves to transform our environment into a pure land because great strength of mind is required. Instead, we imagine that we are in that land and pretend that all appearances are pure. Imagine yourself as Vajrayogini, gazing as if with great desire at Padmasambhava. She wears eight adornments carved from bone and holds a skull cup in her left hand and a carved knife in her right. She stands poised for action in the motion posture. Her body is bright red and non-obstructive; like a rainbow in the sky it appears yet is empty.

One arrow length above her head is a red or otherwise

pleasantly coloured lotus of one hundred thousand petals on which rest cushions of sun and moon discs. Your own lama in the form of the youthful Guru Rin-bo-chay, composite of all the sources of refuge in the past, present and future, sits on the three cushions [lotus, sun and moon]. His body is white with a reddish tinge; he has the clear glowing complexion of an eight- or nine-year-old child. He is seated in the posture of royal ease and wears the same robes described earlier (p. 118). In addition, he has the hat given to him by the King of Zahor, who once attempted to roast Padmasambhava in an oven. When he looked inside, he found Padmasambhava sitting unharmed on a lotus. This caused the king to generate such great faith that he offered Guru Rin-bo-chay his own robe and hat. The hat is called Lotus of Liberation Through Mere Seeing because the sight of it plants the seed of liberation.

The hat is in two layers, symbolizing the unification of the two tantric stages of generation and completion. It has five colours representing the five bodies which bring about the welfare of all sentient beings – the Nature, Wisdom, Enjoyment, Emanation, and Immutable Vajra Bodies. This last is a distillation of the immutable qualities of all Buddha Bodies.

On the front panel of the hat are a sun and moon, symbolizing wisdom and method, while a sky-blue border indicates that Padmasambhava's own vows and promises are limitless as the sky itself. At the top is a vajra ornament, symbol of his immovable meditative stabilization, and a feather that represents his lofty view.

In his right hand, with index finger pointing up, he holds a vajra as a sign that he has subdued all the elements, and in his left a skull containing the vase of long life. This indicates that, as an emanation of Amitayus whose name means 'limitless life,' he has power over life.

A trident before his left shoulder is a sacred symbol of his consort, and its three points symbolize entity, nature and compassion (see p. 120). Three human heads on the trident indicate the Three Buddha Bodies. There are also nine ornaments symbolizing the nine vehicles and five streamers entwined with human hair flowing out from beneath the three heads as emblems of the five wisdoms.

Guru Rin-bo-chay is surrounded by the three sources – lamas, personal deities, and Sky Goers – as well as various other beings. Sustain this visualization while reciting:

E ma ho
In a limitless pure land, spontaneously self-appearing,
Is the full form of the glorious copper-coloured mountain.
In its centre am I as the venerable Vajrayogini
Bright red, with one face and two hands holding a curved knife
  and skull,
With both legs in the motion posture, three eyes looking at the
  sky.
At my crown on top of a thousand-petalled lotus, sun and
  moon
Is the Emanation Body, Padmasambhava, undifferentiable
From my fundamental lama, composite of all sources of refuge,
Of reddish white body and youthful form, wearing
The inner, outer and religious robes and shawl,
In the posture of royal ease, with one face and two hands,
The right hand with a vajra, the left carrying a skull
And vessel, wearing a lotus hat on his head,
Bearing near his left shoulder a trident that indicates
The superior mother of bliss and emptiness.
Sitting amidst a sphere of rainbow rays, drops
And light his retinue appears like clouds in a beautiful
Sky-lattice of five lights, and constitutes the twenty-five
  emanations
Of the master and deputies, Indian and Tibetan scholars
And adepts, Knowledge Bearers, personal gods and deities,
Sky Goers, protectors of religion and bearers of oaths
Vivid in the great equal status of clarity and emptiness.

E ma ho is an expression of wonder at the purity of all that appears. The pure land is said to arise spontaneously because it has not been made from external causes and conditions nor come about through effort and exertion. It is a land of limitless purity, primordially conjoined with suchness, in which all conceptions of subject and object have ceased. No impure objects are to be found and the beings there have completely abandoned all defilements and abide in utter purity.

At the peak of the glorious copper mountain are three mansions. The highest is the abode of the Truth Body, beneath it is the mansion of the Enjoyment Body and below that is Padmasambhava's own marvellous mansion, the abode of the Emanation Body. It is composed of light, and Padmasambhava with many other great adepts sits in a sphere of rainbows and drops of light. Visualize them all as appearing but empty, vivid in the great equal status of clarity and emptiness.

If you are able to visualize the whole spectacle, it is wonderful. If you cannot, just see Guru Rin-bo-chay and invite him to come by reciting:

Hūṃ
At the northwest border of Odiyana,
On the stem of a *kesara* lotus is he
Who attained the amazing supreme siddhi
Known as Padmasambhava, surrounded
By many Sky Goers as his retinue.
I will achieve in accordance with you,
Please come to give blessings and empower me
Guru-padma siddhi hūṃ (O Lotus Guru, pray grant me the
   siddhis).

Hūṃ is a word of invitation meaning, 'Come'. 'Odiyana' is in northwest India, and in its northwest is a lake containing a special lotus of one hundred thousand petals where Padmasambhava abides. Imagine that he comes and blends with his visualized image, like water poured into water. Your visualization then becomes most magnificent, far surpassing its former splendour. Before Guru Rin-bo-chay actually arrived, your mental object was an imagined being; now it is real wisdom being. You ask him for help so that you may become just like him.

Guru padma siddhi hūṃ is a sound inherent in Guru Rin-bo-chay's own heart and comes from him spontaneously. In this case the mantra is not a request, nor is it recited to overcome afflictions; it is the sound of Guru Rin-bo-chay himself, his fundamental mantra.

SEVEN-BRANCHED SERVICE

The seven-branched service is the same as that done at the time of mandala offering (see p. 156). The first branch is obeisance, an antidote to pride:

> *Hrīḥ*
> I bow down with emanations of my body
> As many as the particles of the lands.

Hrīḥ is the heart syllable of all deities of the lotus lineage, including Guru Rin-bo-chay. As you recite the obeisance, emit countless emanations of yourself and cause them all to bow down to the field of assembly, as if you were a prayer-master leading a huge convocation. Your strong feelings of faith and so forth are duplicated in each emanation, and the more of them you are able to visualize the greater the meritorious force will be.

The second branch is offering, an antidote to desire and miserliness:

> I offer through the power of meditation all appearances
> Actually arranged or imagined as Seals of offering.

Offering is made through the power of meditative stabilization, not just with ordinary thought. Offerings physically set out before you are used as a basis for imagination. Mentally multiply them many times and create other varieties as well. In accordance with tantric practice, all appearances of offerings and beings are to be seen as totally pure.

Everything in front of you and that you are capable of imagining is offered to the excellent Guru Rin-bo-chay.

Groups of the five Seals or goddesses – offering forms, sounds, odours, tastes and tangible objects – melt into the Guru, and as each succeeding goddess merges into the corresponding sense organ – eye, ear, nose, tongue, or body – an even greater experience of bliss and emptiness is generated in Guru Rin-bo-chay.

The third branch is confession, an antidote to hatred:

> Within the Truth Body of clear light I confess
> All non-virtuous actions done through the three doors.

The three doors, or modes of activity, are body, speech and mind. All non-virtues necessarily arise from these; therefore at the time of confession you should focus on each one individually. Your confession or revelation is made to the clear light of the Truth Body within an understanding of emptiness. This is the ultimate mode of confession, transcending thought.

The fourth branch is admiration, an antidote to jealousy. Among virtues, there are those associated with conventional truths and those with ultimate truths. At this time you admire and take delight in both:

> I admire all collections of virtue
> That are included within the two truths.

Rejoice in your own and other sentient beings' virtues. It is possible to accumulate an extraordinary amount of meritorious power merely by admiring the virtue of others. In fact, by empathizing with the goodness of a powerfully virtuous person, you yourself acquire merit equalling his.

The fifth branch is an entreaty for the teaching to be given, an antidote to ignorance:

> I request the wheels of teaching of the three vehicles
> To be turned for the trainees of the three lineages.

The trainees of the three lineages are Hearers, Solitary Realizers and Bodhisattvas. After Buddha attained enlightenment, he spent seven weeks in solitary meditation until

Brahma pleaded with him to begin teaching. Until that time Buddha had pretended to have no intention to teach, but at Brahma's request he began to explain doctrine to others.

The sixth branch is an appeal to all great teachers, and particularly Padmasambhava, to remain in the world in order to teach even though they are able to leave cyclic existence entirely. The supplication serves as an antidote to wrong views:

> I beg you to remain without passing away
> Until cyclic existence is emptied [of all beings].

The seventh branch is dedication, an antidote to doubt. By your recitation and meditation you have planted seeds of virtue, and now you make a wish that your past, present and future roots of virtue will grow and bear fruit. You should not wish for worldly wealth or fame but the qualities and situations that will help you attain Buddhahood. Make the dedication in the hope that all your own and others' virtues may ripen into the great enlightenment of a Buddha:

> I dedicate as causes of the great enlightenment
> All virtuous roots amassed in the past, present and future.

SUPPLICATION

Padmasambhava is the quintessence of all gurus. His great qualities are as vast as space and his wisdom, love and power are without obstruction. His compassion rushes forth like a river, filling the hopes of all beings. His mind is immovable like a mountain, and unlike the minds of ordinary beings it is unchangeable. His sustaining love for all is like that of a mother for her own delightful child. Just by seeing, hearing or touching him one can receive the seed of liberation.

If his qualities are related individually by ordinary persons, the telling of them would never be finished. Therefore, with the thought that Guru Rin-bo-chay is the very essence of the compassion and blessings of all Buddhas, request his empowerment with such strong feeling that your hairs stir. Petition earnestly and unwaveringly, offering him everything.

Make the offering without any concern or attachment for body or resources. Feel deeply that Padmasambhava knows all your mental and physical activities, both good and bad, and pray to him to keep watch and bestow whatever help you need. With an intense feeling of admiration and a wish for his protection recite:

> O venerable precious Guru, who is
> The glory containing the compassion
> And blessed empowerment of all Buddhas,
> The sole protector of all sentient beings,
> Without concern I offer to you
> My body, resources, mind, heart and breast.
> From now until attaining enlightenment
> The great venerable Padmasambhava
> Knows all my pleasure, pain, good, bad, high and low.
> *Oṃ āḥ hūṃ vajra-guru-padma siddhi hūṃ.*

The verse is recited three times, and after each one the mantra is repeated a hundred times. Eventually this mantra of twelve syllables is to be recited one hundred thousand times for each syllable – one million two hundred thousand times. This is not difficult; however, for our practice it is appropriate simply to repeat the verse thrice and the mantra a hundred times after each recitation. Then recite:

> For me there is no other place of hope.
> The degenerate living beings of this bad era
> Are sunk in the mud of unbearable suffering,
> Protect us from this, Mahaguru! Bestow the four
> Initiations, bearer of blessed empowerment.
> Flare up our realizations, compassionate one.
> Purify the two obstructions, O powerful one.
> *Oṃ āḥ hūṃ vajra-guru-padma siddhi hūṃ.*

This is a bad era when beings wandering among the six realms are drowning in the mud of unbearable suffering.

You are asking Guru Rin-bo-chay to bestow the four initiations and thereby purify bad actions that give rise to such suffering. You request him to cleanse everything unsuitable in your own and others' continuums and to lift all realizations higher and higher. You ask also that he clear away all obstructions to liberation and to omniscience.

Cease considering yourself to be Vajrayogini and assume your ordinary form. Guru Rin-bo-chay suddenly appears in front of you. The four initiations of Highest Yoga Tantra are received while you visualize and recite the following:

Rays of light emanate from the letter *om* brilliant as crystal between the Guru's eyebrows. These rays penetrate my crown, cleansing physical actions and obstructions of the channels. The blessed empowerment of vajra body enters into me. The vase initiation is attained; I become a vessel for the stage of generation; the seed of a fruition Knowledge Bearer is planted. The lot of attaining the rank of an Emanation Body is set in my mental continuum.

Rays of light emanate from the letter *āḥ*, burning like a red lotus in the Guru's throat and enter mine. They purify verbal actions and obstructions of the winds [energies that course in the channels]. The blessed empowerment of vajra speech enters into me. The secret initiation is attained; I become a vessel for repeating mantras; the seed of a Knowledge Bearer with power over life is planted. The lot of attaining the rank of an Enjoyment Body is established in my mental continuum.

Rays of light the colour of the sky emanate from the letter *hūm* in the Guru's heart and enter mine. They purify mental actions and obstructions of the essential drops. The blessed empowerment of vajra mind enters into me. The wisdom initiation is attained; I become a vessel of the Chandali of bliss and emptiness; the seed of a Seal Knowledge Bearer is planted. The lot of attaining the rank of a Truth Body is established in my mental continuum.

Again from the *hūm* of his heart a second letter *hūm* separates like a shooting star. It mixes undifferentiably with my mind and purifies predispositions in the basis-of-all (*ālaya*) and obstructions to omniscience. The blessed empowerment of vajra wisdom enters into me. The ultimate initiation conveyed by words is attained; I become a vessel of the essentially pure Great Perfection; the seed of a spontaneous Knowledge Bearer is planted. The lot of attaining a Nature Body, the final fruit, is established in my mental continuum.

The brilliant light that emanates from the letter *om̐*, clear as crystal, in the middle of Padmasambhava's forehead enters through an opening in the crown of your head. It cleanses the physical non-virtues of killing, stealing and sexual misconduct. Defects of the [energy or] wind channels in the body are corrected, and later the winds which course in these channels will be purified. For example, the nose passage is first cleared, and then irregular breathing is calmed.

Imagine and believe that a blessed vajra body, immutable and composed of light, is attained. The lot of attaining an Emanation Body is established in you. If you are not too busy, you should pause here, allowing the meaning of this to become clear. Remain in meditative equipoise with the thought that you have actually attained an Emanation Body.

The vase symbolizes the bodies of all Buddhas, and receiving this initiation causes you to attain the rank of an Emanation Body. This is the stage of generating yourself as a deity and your surroundings as his habitat. Through such imagination you will be able so to cleanse the channels in your body that you become capable of physical manifestation at will.

The body that is your present life-support is the fruit of past actions. Similarly, a fruition Knowledge Bearer is the state of purity attained when the mind has ripened into a divine body even though one is still incapable of purifying the physical body.

The letter *āḥ* arises from a collection of channels in Guru Rin-bo-chay's throat. It flames like a red lotus and radiates red light into your throat, purifying verbal actions of lying, harsh speech, divisiveness and foolish talk. Believe that the blessed empowerment of indestructible vajra speech enters you from Guru Padmasambhava. Since a vajra cannot be destroyed by desire, hatred or ignorance, this means that your own speech will not suffer from doubt or pollution. The generators or increasers of speech are winds [or energies] and this initiation, called the secret initiation, purifies all obstructions of them. Through receiving it you become a proper vessel for the repetition of mantra.

At present your life is subject to impermanence. It decreases and diminishes, finally changing into a different type altogether. Through the force of this initiation you attain the seed of a Knowledge Bearer who has power over life, purifying the common body with the fire of meditative stabilization. Thereby, believe that you have actually attained the rank of an Enjoyment Body, the second of the four Buddha Bodies.

Blue light radiates from the blue letter *hūm* abiding in Guru Rin-bo-chay's heart and enters your own. These blue rays purify mental actions – the non-virtuous thoughts of covetousness, harmful intent and wrong views. The rays also purify the refined essence of the body – the essential drops that flow in the channels. Their obstructions are purified, and the blessed empowerment of vajra mind enters into you, causing generation of a mind that cannot be interrupted or affected by afflictions. Thereby the wisdom initiation transforming worldly desires into great bliss is attained. Through receiving it, you become a vessel of the Chandali of bliss and emptiness.

Bliss is generated within the central channel four finger widths below the navel. This is the Chandali, the source of all body warmth. During sexual intercourse the Chandali vibrates a little and great heat arises; the red letter *a* at the Chandali begins to vibrate slightly, causing the heat to move up the central channel and melt a white upside down *ham* near the top of the central channel four finger widths below the crown of the head.

As the heat rises from the *a* shaped nerve centre, it melts a little bit of the white *haṃ*, causing the usual type of male and female pleasure to be generated. In the mantra system, this process of the rising heat is used to generate the four joys. When the heat rising from the letter *a* actually melts part of the *haṃ* and the drops descend to the throat centre, the stage of joy is generated. Sexual pleasure is a mere symbol of the bliss experienced at this time. The duration and strength of this bliss far surpass ordinary sexual experience.

When the drops of the melted *haṃ* arrive at the heart centre, special bliss is experienced. When they arrive at the navel centre, one experiences supreme joy, and when they reach the secret centre, innate joy is generated.

A man who is skilled in this practice does not emit any semen. Instead he draws a refined form of it up through the central channel and spreads it out among the spokes of the channel centres and again generates the four joys. Females generate these joys by drawing a refined element of the menstrual blood up through their central channel. In either sex the ability to move these substances up and down along the central channel requires a great degree of mastery over the winds and a thorough familiarization with the stage of generation. If one is skilled in this practice, no children are conceived. However, union of male and female is not the only way to generate such bliss. Monks and so forth who have taken a vow not to engage in sexual union have methods of accomplishing this practice solely through creative imagination.

As the blue light of the letter *hūṃ* in Guru Rin-bo-chay's heart enters your own, the seed is planted of a Seal Knowledge Bearer – a state corresponding to the second through ninth of the ten Bodhisattva grounds. The Seal is the entity of bliss qualifying everything that appears to the mind, just as a seal leaves an impression in wax. At this time the lot of attaining the rank of a Truth Body is achieved.

From Guru Rin-bo-chay's heart a blue letter *hūṃ* is

emitted like a shooting star. It enters through your heart and mixes undifferentiably with your mind. From that moment Guru Rin-bo-chay's mind is undifferentiable from your own.

The heart is the site of the mind-basis-of-all (*ālayavijñāna*) where all karmic predispositions are stored. When the *hūṃ* letter enters there, all non-virtuous predispositions are purified. Tendencies interfering with the simultaneous cognition of all phenomena in the world systems, known as the obstructions to omniscience, are also purified.

Feel that the blessed empowerment of vajra wisdom has actually entered your continuum. It is not mere imagination but manifest and real. Vajra wisdom is the five Buddha wisdoms, indestructible and incapable of interruption. At this time you also attain the ultimate initiation conveyed by words, so called because words are the means by which its meaning is revealed. Having received this empowerment, you become a vessel for the essentially pure Great Perfection. You become capable of understanding that all phenomena are pure in essence because they have been empty of inherent existence since beginningless time.

The seed of a spontaneous Knowledge Bearer is now planted in you. This Knowledge Bearer is a being whose very nature is a spontaneous effulgence of all marvellous Buddha qualities and thus corresponds to the levels of the path just prior to Buddhahood. The lot of attaining the final fruit, the Nature Body – union of the expanse of suchness and wisdom consciousness – is established in your mental continuum. Then recite:

> When the time of life has passed, relieve
> Me please, O venerable Padma,
> In the land of the Glorious Chamara mountain,
> Self-appearing land of unified emanation.
> May I be transformed into a mass of clear bright light
> With the basic body of Vajrayogini, enlightened
> So that I am undifferentiated
> From the venerable Padmasambhava,

As an excellent captain guiding all beings
In the three realms through the sport of great wisdom,
The artifice of bliss and emptiness.
The petition is made from my heart's centre,
It is not just from the mouth, not just words.
Bestow empowerment from the sphere of your heart,
Pray may the meaning of my thoughts be accomplished.

In petitioning Padmasambhava for relief, you are asking for help in how to end cyclic existence. The copper-coloured mountain where he abides is a land embodying the unification of the two truths: ultimate and conventional, emptiness and appearance. Your expressed hope is that when you die your body will be that of Vajrayogini, a mass of clear light, and that you will become undifferentiable from the venerable Padmasambhava. You would then be a Buddha capable of leading to liberation all sentient beings in the desire, form and formless realms.

This prayer requesting Guru Rin-bo-chay's blessed empowerment should arise not just from your mouth but from the orb of the heart itself. Your petition closes with the wish that these purposes as well as the aims of all sentient beings may be fulfilled.

Guru Rin-bo-chay is so pleased by your request that warm red rays of light spring from his heart. As soon as the rays reach you – now in the form of Vajrayogini – your whole body becomes a mass of red light that contracts to the size of a pea before flying like a spark into Guru Rin-bo-chay's own heart. The spark vanishes in his heart so that you become of one taste and one nature with Guru Rin-bo-chay.

Guru Rin-bo-chay himself dissolves like a rainbow into space, and your mind at that time is one with his in the great expanse. Remain in this state of meditative equipoise for a while. When you arise, think of all appearances as the sport and creations of the lama, the precious Guru.

Close your meditation session by dedicating its value to the welfare of all beings.

O glorious fundamental precious lama,
Residing on the lotus seat in my heart
Take care of me with your great kindness,
Bestow the siddhis of body, speech and mind.

Without generating even for an instant wrong ideas
About the liberation story of the glorious lama
And with respect seeing all his deeds as auspicious,
May the lama's blessed empowerment enter my mind.

This prayer furthers your intention not to engage in faulty notions with regard to anything the lama does. In this way his blessings can enter your mind.

In all births not separate from the true lama
And enjoying the glory of the doctrine, may I
Complete the attributes of the grounds and paths
And quickly attain the rank of Vajradhara.

Through this virtue may all creatures complete
The collections of merit and wisdom
And attain the two excellent bodies
Arising from merit and wisdom.

By the virtue arising from this session of meditation and particularly from the performance of guru yoga may all creatures throughout space complete the conceivable collection of merit and the inconceivable collection of wisdom. May they attain the Form and Truth Bodies that arise respectively from merit and wisdom.

The virtues that all living beings have
Either done, will do or are doing
Are good and so may all in all ways
Become auspicious in the grounds.

Whatever virtues living beings have accomplished in the past, present or future are worthy; therefore, may all sentient beings – not just myself – become accomplished in the Bodhisattva and tantric stages or grounds.

I dedicate all these virtues
Toward my learning in accordance

> With the knowledge of the hero Manjushri
> And likewise of Samantabhadra.

> With the dedications so highly praised
> By all the Conquerors of the three times
> I dedicate to auspicious deeds
> Completely all these roots of virtue.

These dedications are sufficient; however, a special aspirational prayer may be added.

> Wherever I am reborn, may I have
> The seven qualities of high status.
> Right from birth may I meet with the doctrine,
> Having the freedom to achieve it correctly.

> There may I delight an excellent lama,
> Practising doctrine during day and night.
> Realizing and achieving its essential meanings,
> May I cross the ocean of cyclic existence in that life.

> Thoroughly teaching the excellent doctrine in the world
> May I not weary in achieving help for others.
> Through unbiased altruism of great force
> May we all together attain Buddhahood.

A person who is accumulating the preparatory practices repeats the refuge, mind of enlightenment, Vajrasattva and mandala meditations one hundred thousand times. Having completed the four hundred thousand, together with a hundred thousand prostrations to the field of assembly, he becomes a vessel suitable to receive the teachings of breakthrough and leap-over. He continually practises guru yoga, but there is no necessity to complete it one hundred thousand times before being taught the higher path.

My own hope is that any among you who would like to begin the preparatory practices will do so. In that case I will return and teach you the paths of breakthrough and leap-over. As Long-chen-rap-jam has said, no matter how much one likes to stay with friends and acquaintances, when the time comes it is necessary to leave and go elsewhere. With this thought I am leaving. Please keep in mind that I hope to visit you again as soon as it is appropriate.

PART THREE

The Great Perfection

An edited translation of teachings received from
Khetsun Sangpo Rinbochay in Dharmsala, India,
during 1972[34]

The Mahayana doctrines are rare in the world today, but not so rare as the inconceivable quintessential instructions of Secret Mantra, within which those of the Great Perfection are even rarer. It seems that the Great Perfection spread to China because portions of these instructions appear here and there in the literature, but there were no complete translations as in Tibet. In the Tung Huang manuscripts, only an occasional page or two, containing small sections, stanzas and the like, set forth the quintessential instructions of the Great Perfection. There are also a few stanzas on the Vajrasattva repetition according to Ati-Yoga and twenty-five to thirty pages on the Novika Tantras of Maha-Yoga. Based on these, it is clear that the Great Perfection did spread to China and thence to Japan, but only to Tibet was it transmitted in complete form.

In Tibet, before entering the path of breakthrough and leap-over, it was essential to accumulate a hundred thousand refuges, altruistic mind generations, Vajrasattva repetitions, and mandala offerings, as well as to begin one million two hundred thousand guru yogas. No matter who one might be, he had to complete these before hearing anything about the higher path. However, nowadays people are very busy and this doctrine of quintessential instructions is about to disappear. Thus, after long discussion among Nying-ma lamas, we have decided that it would be better to explain this doctrine to interested foreigners. In the past, people were not so busy and were able to climb the ladder, purifying actions and afflictions and making identifications. Now, however, neither the teacher nor the student have the time. If it were strictly held that all of the preparatory practices had to be finished before hearing a word of the higher doctrine, then almost no one could hear it.

If such a profound doctrine of quintessential instructions were to be abandoned, it would be very sad; therefore, at this time of rapid disappearance, as at sunset, it is necessary to reveal the secrets. These instructions will serve as means of completing the potencies of listeners, whereupon it will be realized that initiation is needed in order to ripen the mind and that these quintessential instructions must be sought in detail.

THE VIEW

How is the basis of the Great Perfection identified? It is not sufficient to identify the basis as merely essential purity (*ka dag*) or as only spontaneity (*lhun grub*), but as a union of both. The essential purity is posited from the viewpoint of the mode of being (*gnas lugs*), emptiness; however, unlike the emptiness of annihilation held by the Nihilists, all auspicious attributes are spontaneously established, and from this point of view spontaneity is positive. All virtuous and non-virtuous karmas are planted in this basis-of-all (*ālaya*). When realized, it causes the attainment of Buddhahood; when not, sentient beings wander in cyclic existence. Although it is the basis of error, the error is to be abandoned, not the basis. When a battle is fought, the enemy is to be defeated, not the area of the fight. Similarly, there is no way that this basis could be destroyed. Until it is vividly realized, words are used as signs causing realization, but the words are not the fact.

In Nying-ma, the two aspects of the empty expanse and

wisdom are so completely unified that they do not involve an aggregation (coming together), or separation (dispersal). This union does not need to be newly produced, but has always been; it is unchangeable like a vajra, which is a symbol for that which cannot be symbolized – stable, hard, unobstructible, unchangeable, indestructible and unbreakable.

There are two modes of practice: the sudden and the gradual. The sudden mode is for someone who over many lifetimes has accumulated the proper actions and predispositions, so that when he receives initiation and the lama's identification of reality, he attains high realization. The gradual mode, on the other hand, is not that of the sutra systems in which one achieves enlightenment only after countless aeons of practice, but that of someone on the Mantra path who completes the auspicious qualities, finishing the grounds (*bhūmi*) and paths (*mārga*) gradually even in one lifetime. However, when he identifies reality, he is unable to progress along these paths simultaneously but has to proceed in stages. Thus, even the gradual path is not necessarily long.

When Mi-la-re-ba was first taught the Great Perfection, he thought he could attain Buddhahood without meditation. He remained relaxed without meditating, and thus attained no mental development. Therefore, when his lama tested him and found that he had made no progress, he said, 'I have made a mistake. Though the Great Perfection is indeed inconceivable, you are too lax and not fitted for this easy doctrine. You will have to proceed with great difficulty on the gradual path. Therefore, you should go to the south, consult the translator Mar-ba, and take the difficult path of the gradualist. You have failed at the easy way to Buddhahood.' Thus the lama had to send him away, whereupon Mi-la-re-ba underwent untold difficulties but through the power of devoted effort was able to achieve Buddhahood.

Mi-la-re-ba told his supreme disciple, Gam-bo-ba

(*sGam-po-pa*), who had received all of his teachings, that
upon departure he would bestow his final quintessential
instruction. Gam-bo-ba knew that Mi-la-re-ba had indeed
transmitted all that he had been taught, like pouring from
one pot to another, and wondered what this more profound
doctrine could be. Later when he was about to leave, he
reminded Mi-la-re-ba about this final quintessential
instruction. Mi-la-re-ba said, 'Oh, yes, it is this,' and pulled
up his robe, revealing the cheeks of his buttocks which were
like the hooves of an animal due to his having sat for so long
on stony ground without a cushion. He said, 'My attainment of great realization came from this. You need such
effort, not any other doctrine. This is the essence of my
teaching. Whether you become a Buddha or not depends on
effort. With it there can be no question about your
liberation. Like a son, do what your father says.'

Mindfulness and introspection, impelled by the power of
effort, are the basis of the path. Mindfulness keeps one from
forgetting what is to be adopted or discarded, and introspection causes one to recognize deviations from the path.
Since this is the case, whether one is eating, lying down,
working, going out, or whatever, if mindfulness and
introspection do not remain tightly in the mind, then there
is no way to tell the difference between an ordinary person
and a practitioner. The division is not made by clothing but
by the mind; clothes do not achieve Buddhahood, the mind
does. Mindfulness and introspection must be maintained
tightly and continuously; otherwise, whether one studies or
practises, one is not on the path.

What is the sudden mode of practice? Here it is not
necessary to complete the visualization of oneself as a deity
with specific symbols and so forth; also there is no need to
bring to fulfilment, through depending on the wisdom
stage of completion, the knowledge of the mode of being –
emptiness. Rather, the student's predispositions from
former actions are activated by the words of his lama such
as:

By the force of knowledge and non-knowledge
If this is known, a Buddha, and if not,
A sentient being wanders in cyclic existence.

If through such quintessential instructions one can identify the basis of the mind, then in that instant one has become a Buddha without engaging in the difficulties of the gradual path. Among a hundred thousand trainees there are only one or two such persons and thus although they do occur, they are very rare.

The student must have accumulated actions and pre-dispositions for many lifetimes, and the lama must have great realization and attainment. When the two sit down to identify the Great Perfection, the student is an ordinary being, but upon identifying his own mind he is freed, and when he arises he is a Superior (*Āryan*). This is because the difference between an ordinary being and a Superior comes only from whether one does or does not know the mode of being of one's own mind. An individual who is capable of being freed immediately on being given the lama's quintessential instruction is called a simultaneous person. If this does not happen, one enters the gradual way, developing the mind in stages over many months, proceeding over the various grounds and paths, whereas those whose mode of progress is sudden realize that the mode of being of their mind is free from the very beginning.

Then, why is it that we are ordinary beings? Because of the obstruction by temporary adventitious defilements. Why are we not freed immediately? Because apart from a general image, we cannot realize this mode of being directly. For instance, one can understand something about a distant city that one does not know by hearing about it, but because one cannot see it directly, it is only an understanding. Those able to take the sudden path, on the other hand, do not just understand the mode of being of the mind, they perceive it directly upon the lama's identification, feeling, 'It's pathetic, I have made such a small mistake, yet have to undergo this huge error of

limitless cyclic existence with so much suffering!' There is
only a small difference between knowing and not knowing,
but the resultant error is huge since birth in cyclic existence
has no beginning.

It is said in Atisha's biography that every day he saw a
woman who was at times crying and at others laughing.
Finally he asked her, 'Why is it that for no apparent reason
you sometimes cry and sometimes laugh? Are you in any
way mentally distressed?'

'No. I am not. You people are and so I cry.'

Why?'

'The Tathagata essence, one's own mind, has been a
Buddha from beginningless time. By not knowing this,
great complications follow from such a small base of error
for hundreds of thousands of sentient beings. Although
their own minds are Buddhas, they are in such great
confusion. Not being able to bear the suffering of so many
beings, I cry. And then, I laugh because when this small
basis of error is known – when one knows one's own mind
– one is freed. Enjoying the fact that sentient beings can so
easily be released from suffering, I laugh, knowing that they
are ready to be liberated.'

She was identifying the base for him. Having penetrat-
ingly realized this basis, the person on the sudden path
immediately moves on to Buddhahood without relying on
entering the gradual path in order to realize his potencies.
However, if one does not succeed on the sudden path, it
is necessary to change to the gradual. Here one trains
externally in the mode of appearance of the expanse of
emptiness and perfects internally the wisdom consciousness, increasing the necessary factors and realizing their
potencies.

The expanse of emptiness and wisdom are the basis of
liberation. The external expanse is that of the sky; the
internal one is the empty sphere of the mind; the secret
expanse is the wisdom mind freed from all extremes once
the mind has been purified. In Madhyamika this is called the

freedom from all conceptual elaborations without anything to point to and with the eight extremes, of production from self, other, both, and neither, coming, going, sameness and difference, refuted – a complete cessation of all elaborations. This inconceivable emptiness, having passed beyond all conceptuality, is the Madhyamika view free from elaborations, which in Mantra is identified through a process beginning with the lama's pointing out and one's identifying one's own mind.

Just after completing the preparatory practices, one examines from where the mind arises, then where it dwells, and finally into what it ceases. These are called the arising, dwelling, and going of the mind. At first one thinks solely about what mind is and from where it comes, without any further instruction, seeking the place of its arising. Then, once one has understood that mind is something that cannot become entirely nonexistent, for it is happy, sad, desirous, hateful and so forth – once it is understood as existing – one examines the upper, middling and lower parts of the body for its home, since it is not suitable for it to dwell in external phenomena. After spending a month or two in this search with great intensity in solitary retreat, one understands that mind has no dwelling place in the body, though for a time it appears to be here or there. Then, since last year's or yesterday's mind does not exist today, one examines where it disappeared and went. What is the entity of the place of cessation of this mind that ceases and is forgotten? At this point one arrives at something that is empty, and when this has to a certain degree been understood, the teaching of breakthrough is begun.

Once the eight extremes are stopped, this empty expanse which is the mode of being of the mind is identified not merely as like space, but as an entity of wisdom, with all the auspicious attributes of knowledge, mercy and power spontaneously established. If everything were considered to be conceptually elaborative and were denied, concluding that all is nonexistent, then what would be the point of practice? The great wisdom that spontaneously has the Buddha qualities of knowledge, mercy and power is identified by the lama, after which one must keep to this path through mindfulness and introspection and thereby advance to Buddhahood. Unless one proceeds in this way, external rearrangements – such as changes in clothing and so forth – cannot bring about Buddhahood. However this does not mean that artificial practices are not to be done. Until the doctrine which the lama reveals has been actualized, effort and exertion in mindfulness and introspection are absolutely essential. Without them, the true essence is lost.

By relying on mindfulness and introspection, the potencies of wisdom are gradually fulfilled like a moon shining in darkness, shining forth from within, not from the outside; knowledge then dawns unimpeded. All phenomena asserted as conventional or ultimate are simultaneously freed, whereupon the realization of the great self-liberation is generated. At that time, one effortlessly attains the great Buddhahood, the expanse of emptiness and the wisdom of self-liberation.

No matter how many or what type of external objects appear, because internal appearances have been brought to fulfilment, there is no more attachment. Grasping is not involved because all conceptual elaborations have been eliminated; the source of a sense of subject (apprehender) and object (apprehended) has been concluded. Because a wisdom beyond stoppage and achievement has appeared from within, there is nothing to be either abandoned or achieved; one is beyond the external subjects and objects of adoption and abandonment.

The auspicious attributes of a Buddha are spontaneously established in the union of the expanse of profound emptiness and wisdom. Just as a snake that has been tied tightly into many knots can free itself, so can the mind undo its own knots. If knots are tied in a rope, someone is needed to unravel them; however the knots of contaminated actions, afflictions and predispositions tied over many lifetimes can be undone like those of a snake. When this is known, one is a Buddha, and when unknown, one wanders in cyclic existence. In itself it is beyond both cyclic existence and nirvana. One has arrived at a high place where the elaborations of these two are eliminated. Since the auspicious attributes of a Buddha have been perfected from within, how could one be reborn in cyclic existence? Since the potencies of the wisdom of a Buddha have been completed, what need is there to follow the path of solitary peace in the Hinayana? This path which takes countless aeons in the sutra system can be accomplished by one mind untying its own knots. It is decided from within.

The waves of conceptual thought subside naturally. Unobstructed and empty, but without being overextended, this state of union is blissful. Union is inherent, not something new joined to something old. The self-arisen nature of phenomena is understood to be free from views. The expanse of emptiness and wisdom are not overly vast and thereby lacking the spontaneous establishment of the qualities of a Buddha. They are not extended to the point where they need to be pieced back together; nor are they partial since they are the one pervasive sphere of the Buddha wisdom, the one great spontaneous pervasive entity. This union has existed from the very beginning, obscured by actions and predispositions which when peeled away leave just this immutable view.

Though the mode of being can be pointed out with words, actualization of it is not a case of thinking about the meaning of words. Still, in dependence on these verbal symbols the mode of being of one's mind can become manifest.

When one gains initiation and transmission of the quintessential instruction and then retreats to a solitary place, one can have these experiences oneself. Precepts not understood when read from books are cognized immediately, for one is then proceeding on the basis of internal knowledge. Then, when one dies, it will be like returning home to one's mother, without the smallest worry.

PART FOUR

Daily Recitation and Meditation

Being a translation of Jik-may-ling-ba's *Recitation of the Preliminaries to the Heart Essence of Vast Openness, Illuminating the Good Path to Omniscience,* with a practical introduction by Khetsun Sangpo Rinbochay

As soon as you awaken in the morning, imagine that Padmasambhava with his retinue of deities and Bodhisattvas appear vividly before you, ringing bells and beating small drums.[35] Their music dispels all drowsiness, rousing you into complete wakefulness.

Next, in order to expel contrary winds [energies] from the body, engage in a purifying breathing practice. Imagine that blessings in the form of white light stream down from Padmasambhava and his retinue and enter your left nostril. Stretch out your left hand in front and draw the light towards your left nostril with your forefinger as an indication that you are drawing their blessings in through your nose. Imagine that you are breathing only through your left nostril and that the light inhaled fills your whole body. It drives out all hatred, which very forcefully is blown out through your right nostril in the form of a light brown snake that disappears in the far distance.

Take the next breath through your right nostril, drawing in the white light of blessing with the index finger of your right hand. The light again fills your body, this time driving out all desire in the form of a dark red cock. This is expelled through your left nostril with a quiet breath and quickly vanishes into distant space.

Inhale the white light of blessings through both nostrils, using both forefingers to draw it in. The light descends through the left and right channels and then returns up the central channel, driving out all ignorance in the form of a grey pig. The pig is expelled with a moderate exhalation and you imagine that it leaves through the crown of your head. The snake, cock and pig are formed by collecting the poisons of desire, hatred and ignorance from every part of your body, and the exhalations expel them from your mental continuum. The series is repeated three times for the purpose of expelling the coarse, middling and subtle forms of hatred, desire and ignorance.

Imagine a flaming red *ram* at the root of your tongue. In some sessions think of it as very small, in others as quite large. Its colour becomes brighter and brighter, and as your tongue is burned up by its fire, feel that all karmic obstructions of speech are utterly consumed and cleared away. In place of your tongue, which has been burned away completely, a three-spoked golden vajra with a reddish tinge appears. Three concentric circles of letters form around the middle of the vajra. The inner one is composed of the Sanskrit vowels, symbolizing wisdom, the middle one of consonants, symbolizing method, and the outer circle is the mantra called 'essence of dependent-arising,' as it contains the meaning of the profound teaching of dependent-arising. Buddha, the great practitioner of virtue, related the paths overcoming suffering and thereby its cessation. He gave eighty-four thousand types of doctrine and their essence is contained in the teaching of the dependent-arising of all phenomena. The import of this arising is that things do not exist in and of themselves inherently.

The essence of dependent-arising mantra is recited in Sanskrit because the language contains special blessings, and through repeating it predispositions for learning Sanskrit are established. However English or Tibetan letters may also be used.

In the morning, recite the alphabet and mantra seven times, omitting the final word, '*svāhā*,' which means, 'So be it'. At night, complete the mantra you began in the morning by saying '*svāhā*' when your head touches the pillow. The mantra imparts a blessed empowerment to your tongue and speech. As you recite it, visualize rays of light spreading out from the letters in your mouth. Goddesses at the ends of the rays make marvellous offerings to the Buddhas and Bodhisattvas. Like snow melting into a lake, the kindness and blessings of the Buddhas and Bodhisattvas merge into the rays of light which then return to you and bless your own faculty of speech.

EMPOWERING BLESSINGS FOR SPEECH

Recite:

Om āh hūm
Fire arises from the letter *ram* and consumes the tongue.
Around the vowels and consonants in the centre
Of a three-spoked vajra of red light
Is the heart of dependent-arising.
From the letters like a pearl rosary, light spreads
Pleasing the Conquerors and their Children with offerings.
Again gathering and purifying obstructions of speech.
I thereby obtain all blessings and siddhis of vajra speech.

Recite seven times:

A ā, i ī, u ū, ri rī, li lī, e ai, o au, am ah
ka kha ga gha na
cha chha ja jha ña
ta tha da dha na
ta tha da dha na
pa pha ba bha ma
ya ra la va
sha sha sa ha kshah
Ye dharma-hetu-prabhavā hetum teshām tathāgato hyavadat
teshām cha yo nirodha evam vādī mahāshramanah svāhā.

About those phenomena [true sufferings] arising from causes [true sources – contaminated actions and afflictions] the Tathagata related the causes [overcoming them – true paths] and thus the Great Practitioner of Virtue related their cessation [the true cessation of sufferings and their sources], so be it.[36]

PETITIONING TO STIR THE GLORIOUS LAMA'S MIND

Say with strong feeling:

> The lama knows. The lama knows. The lama knows.[37]
> O kind lama, sole refuge, open the lotus
> Of faith in the centre of my heart and rise up.
> Reside as an adornment of the great wheel of bliss
> At the crown of my head to protect me, the undeserving
> Troubled with polluted actions and strong afflictions.
> Please arouse all my mindfulness and awareness.

DIFFICULTY OF FINDING OPPORTUNITIES AND CONDITIONS

Recite:

> I have now attained an opportunity free from the eight
> Impediments – hell-being, hungry ghost, animal,
> A god of long life, barbarian, holding wrong views,
> A Buddha not coming, and stupidity.

> I have all five inner conditions – human life,
> Full faculties, birth in a central land,
> Not having done horrible deeds, and faith
> In the teaching. I have the five outer conditions –
> A Buddha's coming, his teaching doctrine,
> The teaching remaining, my entry into it,
> And aid from an excellent spiritual guide.

> Though I have attained a state with all these features,
> Giving up this uncertain life with many causes
> Of death I will go to the next transitory life.
> Transform my attitudes into practice, the guru knows.
> Let me not go on low wrong paths, O omniscient leader.
> You differ not at all from them, the kind lama knows.

If now I do not make meaningful this supporting
    opportunity,
Later I will not find a base to achieve liberation.
Consuming merit on this base of a happy life,
After death I will wander in a lower realm,
Not knowing virtue and sin, not hearing the sounds of
    doctrine,
Not meeting with a spiritual guide – it will be full of horror.

If I think of the number and levels of sentient beings,
I realize the attainment of a human body is rare.
If I think of humans without religion involved in sins,
Those who practise a religion are like stars during the day.
Transform my attitudes into practice, the guru knows.
Let me not go on low wrong paths, O omniscient leader.
You differ not at all from them, the kind lama knows.

I have arrived in a precious place where I have a human
    body,
Thus my physical base is fortunate but an ordinary mind
Is not well suited for achieving liberation.
In particular there are the eight sudden impediments –
Control by an evil one, disturbance by the five poisons,
Interruption by bad karma, distraction by laziness,
Slavery to others, seeking religion for protection from
    fear,

Pretension of being a practitioner, and obscuration.
When for me these become contraries to practice,
Transform my attitudes into practice, the guru knows.
Let me not go on low wrong paths, O omniscient leader.
You differ not at all from them, the kind lama knows.

The eight impediments of a depriving mind are to have
Little disgust for cyclic existence, separation
From the wealth of faith, binding by the noose of attachment,
Rough behaviour, not shunning non-virtues, turning away
From practice, losing vows, and destroying pledges.
When for me these become contraries to practice,
Transform my attitudes into practice, the guru knows.
Let me not go on low wrong paths, O omniscient leader.
You differ not at all from them, the kind lama knows.

IMPERMANENCE OF LIFE

Now I am not troubled by sickness and suffering,
I have freedom, not controlled by others like a slave.
If now when these dependent-arisings coincide
I waste my opportunities and conditions in idleness,
What need to say about companions, friends, enjoyments
And relatives, even this body I hold so dear
Will be taken from my bed to a barren spot
And torn apart by wolves, vultures and jackals.
The fear in the bardo will be extremely great.
Transform my attitudes into practice, the guru knows.
Let me not go on low wrong paths, O omniscient leader.
You differ not at all from them, the kind lama knows.

FAULTS OF CYCLIC EXISTENCE AND CAUSE
AND EFFECT OF ACTIONS

The fruition of virtuous and sinful deeds will follow later.
In particular, if I go to the transient worlds of the hells,
There is one group of eight where my head and body
Are rent by weapons on a field of burning iron,
Are cut by a saw, smashed by a red hot hammer,
Enclosed in a doorless iron house, crying, impaled
On a heated pitchfork, boiled in molten bronze,
Or burned by searing fire of extreme heat.

There is another group of eight lands –
On the surface of dense mountains of snow
And frightful narrow ways of ice, dry
Snowstorms and cold winds batter my body
Making blisters and also those that burst.
Always moaning and with pain hard to bear,
My strength is spent; like the sick near death
I groan long and hard, my teeth chatter,
My skin splits and the exposed flesh splits more.

Passing through the hells near the most tortuous,
My feet are cut on a plain of razors,
My body is cut and sliced in a grove of swords,
I enter into the mud of putrid corpses
And into the centre of burning hot ashes.

I become like a door, post, stove, rope, and so forth
In the trifling hells of continual misuse.

These are the eighteen forms of hell, and when
A motivation of strong hatred arises
Making the causes from which the hells appear,
Transform my attitudes into practice, the guru knows.
Let me not go on low, wrong paths, O omniscient leader.
You differ not at all from them, the kind lama knows.

In a poor and ugly land the names of food, drink
And resources are not even heard. The hungry ghosts,
Dried out and with little strength to stand erect,
Do not obtain food and drink for months and years.
Miserliness is the cause creating their three types.

Animals eat each other, frightened of being killed,
Stricken by being used for other's purposes,
And too muddled to know what to adopt or discard.
The seed of such endless suffering is ignorance.
When I wander in the darkness of that ignorance,
Transform my attitudes into practice, the guru knows.
Let me not go on low wrong paths, O omniscient leader.
You differ not at all from them, the kind lama knows.

Engaging in practice, but not binding bad deeds,
Entering the door of Mahayana, yet not having an attitude of
   helping others,
Attaining the four initiations, without cultivating generation
   and completion,
May the lama free me from these mistaken paths.

Though not realizing the view, having haughty behaviour,
Though distracted in meditation, bragging to others,
Though mistaken in behaviour, not thinking of my own faults,
May the lama liberate me from this dislike for practice.

Though dying the next morning, attached to home, clothing
   and wealth,
Though losing youth, not disgusted or thinking to renounce,
Though having heard little, claiming to be learned,
May the lama free me from this ignorance.

Though about to fall into bad circumstances, thinking of the
hurly-burly,
Though staying in solitary retreat, being rigid in mind like a
tree,
Though claiming to be disciplined, not destroying hatred and
desire,
May the lama liberate me from these eight practices of the
world.
Please wake me quickly from this heavy sleep,
Please remove me quickly from this dark prison.

REFUGE

Until [manifesting] the essence of enlightenment I go for
refuge
To the actuality of the Three Jewels, the three sources [which
are a composite of all] Sugatas
To the mind of enlightenment which has the nature of the
channels, winds and drops [purified as the Three Bodies],
And to the mandala of entity, nature and compassion.[38]

GENERATION OF AN ALTRUISTIC ASPIRATION TO HIGHEST ENLIGHTENMENT

Hoh

I am generating an altruistic mind of enlightenment
Within the four immeasurables so that living beings
Who wander up and down the chain of cyclic existence
Because of false images like those cast by the moon in water,
May rest in the sphere of self-knowledge and clear light.

VAJRASATTVA MEDITATION AND REPETITION

Āh

Above the crown of my own normal head
Are cushions of a white lotus and a moon.
From the *hūm* in their centre Vajrasattva appears
With the clear white body of Complete Enjoyment
Holding vajra and bell and embracing his consort.

I ask you for refuge and to cleanse my sins, confessed
With a strong mind of contrition. Henceforth
I will refrain from them though it cost my life.
On your heart's broad moon is the letter *hūm*
Surrounded by the mantra. Through repeating
This mantra your continuum is stirred, and from the place
Of union of the father and mother's blissful sport
Comes the cloud of the nectar of the mind of
  enlightenment,
Falling like drops of camphor. Through it may all polluted
Actions and afflictions which cause all suffering,
Sickness, spirits, sins, obstructions, faults, infractions,
And defilements of myself and all beings
In the three realms be made completely clean.

Repeat as many times as possible:

Om Vajrasattva, samayam anupālaya, Vajrasattva, tvenopatiṣhṭha, dṛdho me bhava, sutoṣnyo me bhava, supoṣnyo me bhava, anurakto me bhava, sarva-siddhim me prayachchha, sarva-karmasu cha me chittam shrīyam kuru, hūm ha ha ha ha hoḥ, Bhagavan-sarva-tathāgata-vajra, mā me muñcha, vajrī bhava, mahāsamaya-sattva, āḥ hūm (Om Vajrasattva, keep [your] pledge. Vajrasattva, reside [in me]. Make me firm. Make me satisfied. Fulfil me. Make me compassionate. Grant me all feats. Also, make my mind virtuous in all actions. *Hūm ha ha ha ha hoḥ* all the blessed Tathagatas, do not abandon me, make me indivisible. Great Pledge Being, *āḥ hūm.*)

Recite:

O protector, through ignorance I have
Contradicted and broken my pledges.
May I be guarded by the lama protector!
I take refuge in the leader of living beings
The leader holding a vajra
Whose nature is great compassion.

I earnestly confess all pollution of my pledges of body, speech and mind – fundamental and secondary. Please cleanse and purify all my masses of defilement – sins, obstructions, faults and infractions.

Pleased and smiling, Vajrasattva grants, 'O child of good lineage, all your sins, obstructions, faults and infractions are purified.'

He melts into light, and through dissolving into me, I too become Vajrasattva, appearing and empty, like an image in a mirror. Light emanates from the four sets of letters around the *hūṃ*, the heart life. The beings of the three realms along with all environments become fully enlightened into the nature of beings and environments of the five Vajrasattva lineages.

Repeat as much as possible:

Oṃ Vajrasattva hūṃ

Set yourself in meditative equipoise.

MANDALA

Recite:

Oṃ āḥ hūṃ
Through offering in full the lands of a thousand million world
    systems
Each having a thousand million worlds, filled with the seven
    precious substances
And wealth of gods and humans, as well as my body and
    resources,
May I attain the reign of a universal monarch of doctrine.

Through offering a heavily adorned highest pure land of great
    bliss
With the five definite attributes and groups of the five lineages
And inconceivable cloud masses of desirable offerings,
May I come to make use of the pure land of an Enjoyment
    Body.

Through offering pure appearances and beings, the encased
    youthful body,
The adornment of sport in reality with unimpeded
    compassion,
A land purified of apprehension of body and drops,[39]
May I come to make use of the land of a Body of Truth.

CUTTING ATTACHMENT

A Beggar's Amassing of the Collections of Merit

Phaṭ

No longer cherishing the body, the god demon [of distraction]
    is overcome.
The mind emerges into the expanse of space through the
    Brahma opening,
Overcoming the death-lord demon and turning into the fierce
    goddess.
Her left hand holds a skull as an instrument and her right
A curved knife conquering the demon of afflictions, cutting off
The skull and overcoming the demon of the form
    aggregate.
She sets it on a hearth of human skulls which form the Three
    Bodies.
Inside it the corpse filling the thousand million worlds is
    distilled
Into pure nectar by the syllables, *a* and *haṃ*,
And is purified, increased and transformed
By the power of the three syllables.

Repeat for as long as seems appropriate:

Oṃ āḥ hūṃ

Recite:

Phaṭ

Offerings are made to the high guests and their intentions are
    fulfilled.
Masses of merit completed, I attain the common and supreme
    siddhis.
The low guests of cyclic existence are pleased and all my debts
    are cleared,
Especially all those who harm and obstruct are well satisfied,
Sicknesses, spirits and interruptors vanish in the expanse,
Bad circumstances and selfishness are all reduced to dust.
At last all that is left of the offerings and recipients
Is the unfabricated *a* in the Great Perfection nature.

GURU YOGA

Recite and visualize:

E ma ho
In a limitless pure land, spontaneously self-appearing,
Is the full form of the glorious copper-coloured mountain.
In its centre am I as the venerable Vajrayogini
Bright red, with one face and two hands holding a curved knife
    and skull,
With both legs in the motion posture, three eyes looking at the
    sky.
At my crown on top of a thousand-petalled lotus, sun and moon,
Is the Emanation Body, Padmasambhava, undifferentiable
From my fundamental lama, composite of all sources of refuge,
Of reddish white body and youthful form, wearing
The inner, outer and religious robes and shawl,
In the posture of royal ease, with one face and two hands,
The right hand with a vajra, the left carrying a skull
And vessel, wearing a lotus hat on his head,
Bearing near his left shoulder a trident that indicates
The superior mother of bliss and emptiness.
Sitting amidst a sphere of rainbow rays, drops
And light his retinue appears like clouds in a beautiful
Sky-lattice of five lights, and constitutes the twenty-five
    emanations
Of the master and deputies, Indian and Tibetan scholars
And adepts, Knowledge Bearers, personal gods and deities,
Sky Goers, protectors of religion and bearers of oaths
Vivid in the great equal status of clarity and emptiness.

Hūṃ
At the northwest border of Odiyana,
On the stem of a *kesara* lotus is he
Who attained the amazing supreme siddhi
Known as Padmasambhava, surrounded
By many Sky Goers as his retinue.
I will achieve in accordance with you,
Please come to give blessings and empower me
Guru-padma siddhi hūṃ (O Lotus Guru, pray grant me the
    siddhis).

Hriḥ

I bow down with emanations of my body
As many as the particles of the lands.

I offer through the power of meditation all appearances
Actually arranged or imagined as Seals of offering.

Within the Truth Body of clear light I confess
All non-virtuous actions done through the three doors.

I admire all collections of virtue
That are included within the two truths.

I request the wheels of teaching of the three vehicles
To be turned for the trainees of the three lineages.

I beg you to remain without passing away
Until cyclic existence is emptied [of all beings].

I dedicate as causes of the great enlightenment
All virtuous roots amassed in the past, present and future.

With strong feeling and belief stirring mind and body recite:

O venerable precious Guru, who is
The glory containing the compassion
And blessed empowerment of all Buddhas,
The sole protector of all sentient beings,
Without concern I offer to you
My body, resources, mind, heart and breast.
From now until attaining enlightenment
The great venerable Padmasambhava
Knows all my pleasure, pain, good, bad, high and low.

Recite one hundred times:

Oṃ āḥ hūṃ vajra-guru-padma siddhi hūṃ

With strong feeling and belief stirring the mind and body recite:

For me there is no other place of hope.
The degenerate living beings of this bad era
Are sunk in the mud of unbearable suffering,

Protect us from this, Mahaguru! Bestow the four
Initiations, bearer of blessed empowerment,
Flare up our realizations, compassionate one.
Purify the two obstructions, O powerful one.[40]

Recite one hundred times:

Oṃ āḥ hūṃ vajra-guru-padma siddhi hūṃ

Recite and visualize:

Rays of light emanate from the letter *oṃ* brilliant as crystal
between the Guru's eyebrows. These rays penetrate my crown,
cleansing physical actions and obstructions of the channels. The
blessed empowerment of vajra body enters into me. The vase
initiation is attained; I become a vessel for the stage of
generation; the seed of a fruition Knowledge Bearer is planted.
The lot of attaining the rank of an Emanation Body is set in my
mental continuum.

Rays of light emanate from the letter *āḥ* burning like a red lotus
in the Guru's throat and enter mine. They purify verbal actions
and obstructions of the winds [energies that course in the
channels]. The blessed empowerment of vajra speech enters
into me. The secret initiation is attained; I become a vessel for
repeating mantras; the seed of a Knowledge Bearer with power
over life is planted. The lot of attaining the rank of an
Enjoyment Body is established in my mental continuum.

Rays of light the colour of the sky emanate from the letter *hūṃ*
in the Guru's heart and enter mine. They purify mental actions
and obstructions of the essential drops. The blessed empowerment of vajra mind enters into me. The wisdom initiation is
attained; I become a vessel of the Chandali of bliss and
emptiness; the seed of a Seal Knowledge Bearer is planted. The
lot of attaining the rank of a Truth Body is established in my
mental continuum.

Again from the *hūṃ* of his heart a second letter *hūṃ* separates
like a shooting star. It mixes undifferentiably with my mind
and purifies predispositions in the basis-of-all (*ālaya*) and
obstructions to omniscience. The blessed empowerment of
vajra wisdom enters into me. The ultimate initiation conveyed
by words is attained; I become a vessel of the essentially pure

Great Perfection; the seed of a spontaneous Knowledge Bearer is planted. The lot of attaining a Nature Body, the final fruit, is established in my mental continuum.

When the time of life has passed, relieve
Me please, O venerable Padma,
In the land of the glorious Chamara mountain
Self-appearing land of unified emanation.
May I be transformed into a mass of clear bright light,
With the basic body of Vajrayogini, enlightened
So that I am undifferentiated
From the venerable Padmasambhava,
As an excellent captain guiding all beings
In the three realms through the sport of great wisdom,
The artifice of bliss and emptiness.
The petition is made from my heart's centre,
It is not just from the mouth, not just words.
Bestow empowerment from the sphere of your heart,
Pray may the meaning of my thoughts be accomplished.

Warm rays of light suddenly arise from the Guru's heart. While visualizing myself as Vajrayogini the warmth merely touches my heart, and I turn into a mass of red light, dissolving into the precious Guru's heart. Thereby I become undifferentiably of one taste with the precious Guru.

Through this union of recitation and meditation, the initiations are attained. After that your body, speech and mind scatter like sparks and mix with the lama's body, speech and mind in the heart of the precious Guru Padmasambhava. Within freedom from imagination, thought and speech set yourself in meditative equipoise.

PETITIONING THE LINEAGE OF FUNDAMENTAL AND INDIRECT LAMAS WITH MINDFULNESS OF THEIR ATTRIBUTES

Recite:

E ma ho

To the primordial Buddha, the Truth Body, Samantabhadra arisen

From the realm free of annihilated expanse and partiality,
To the Enjoyment Body Vajrasattva with the sport and
    potency of a moon in water,
To Ga-rap-dor-jay fully endowed as an Emanation Body
I pray, bestow blessed empowerment and initiation.

To Shrisimha, treasury of the ultimate doctrine,
To Manjushrimitra, universal monarch of the nine vehicles,
To Jnanasutra, and to the great pandita Vimalamitra
I pray, teach the various paths of liberation.

To Padmasambhava, sole adornment of this world,
And the superior sons of his heart, the master, deputies and
    friend,[41]
To the revered Long-chen-rap-jam, who reveals the meaning
    of the mind treasure ocean,
To Jik-may-ling-ba, transmitter of the Sky Goers' sphere
    treasury
I pray, bestow the attainment of the fruit, liberation.

To the great Knowledge Bearer, Gyel-way-nyu-gu,
To the honorable Ba-drul Jik-may-chö-gi-wang-bo,
To Shen-pen-nang-way-bel, scholar and adept,
To Jam-yang-wang-gyel, and my fundamental lamas
I pray, bestow the common and superior siddhis.

Through the blessed empowerment of these petitions
May conditions against achieving the doctrine be pacified,
May I quickly progress on the path of the four Knowledge
    Bearers,[42]
Quickly attaining the rank of the Four Buddha Bodies.

With the disgust of wanting to leave cyclic existence
I will rely on the precious vajra lama as an eye.
Through constant effort at achievement, not laying aside
The profound practices for achieving the word you speak,
May the empowerment of your continuum be transferred.

May manifest reality nakedly be seen,
The Great Perfection free of adopting, discarding, activity and
    effort,
The tone of mind passed beyond knowledge, vision,
    conception and investigation.

The fruit of completing [all ordinary appearance and adherence
    to ordinariness] as a deity, purifying [all sounds] as mantra,
    and ripening [all conceptions] as the Truth Body
[Since] appearances, occurrences, cyclic existence, and nirvana
    are from the start Highest Pure Lands.
May thoughts of true existence be freed, and visionary
    experience
Of bodies and drops in the centre of rainbow rays be enhanced,
May the potency of mind be fulfilled as the land of the
    Enjoyment Body,
May Buddhahood be realized in the great beyond-mind of
    extinguishment
In reality, gaining finality as the encased youthful body.

If I do not succeed in experiencing the great yoga
And this coarse body is not freed in the essential expanse,
Then when the factors of this life are ending, may the clear light
Of death appear as the essentially pure Body of Truth,
May bardo appearances be freed as an Enjoyment Body,
And fulfilling the path potencies of breakthrough and leap-over
May I be liberated like a child set on his mother's lap.

If I am not freed in the manifest original ground,
The great secret clear light, peak of supreme vehicles,
Face of the Truth Body not sought from other Buddhas,
May I, depending on the supreme path of the five doctrines
    without meditation,
Be relieved by the Odiyana leader – supreme in the ocean of
    Knowledge Bearers.

May I be born as the chief son in the rank of a disseminator
Of the feast of great secret doctrine in naturally emanated
Five lands and especially in the lotus light palace
As a source of sustenance for limitless living beings.

Through the blessed empowerment of the Knowledge Bearers,
    the oceanic conquerors,
And through the truth of the inconceivable expanse of reality
May I on this base of leisure and fortune actualize the
    dependent-arising
Of completion, ripening, and purification and so attain
    Buddhahood.

DEDICATION

O glorious fundamental precious lama,
Residing on the lotus seat in my heart
Take care of me with your great kindness,
Bestow the siddhis of body, speech and mind.

Without generating even for an instant wrong ideas
About the liberation story of the glorious lama
And with respect seeing all his deeds as auspicious,
May the lama's blessed empowerment enter my mind.

In all births not separate from the true lama
And enjoying the glory of doctrine, may I
Complete the attributes of the grounds and paths
And quickly attain the rank of Vajradhara.

Through this virtue may all creatures complete
The collections of merit and wisdom
And attain the two excellent bodies
Arising from merit and wisdom.

The virtues that all living beings
Either have done, will do or are doing
Are good and so may all in all ways
Become auspicious in the grounds.

I dedicate all these virtues
Toward my learning in accordance
With the knowledge of the hero Manjushri
And likewise of Samantabhadra.

With the dedications so highly praised
By all the Conquerors of the three times
I dedicate to auspicious deeds
Completely all these roots of virtue.

SPECIAL ASPIRATIONAL PRAYER

Wherever I am reborn, may I have
The seven qualities of high status.
Right from birth may I meet with the doctrine,
Having the freedom to achieve it rightly.

There may I delight an excellent lama,
Practising doctrine during day and night.
Realizing and achieving its essential meanings,
May I cross the ocean of cyclic existence in that life.

Thoroughly teaching the excellent doctrine in the world
May I not weary in achieving help for others.
Through unbiased altruism of great force
May we all together attain Buddhahood.

Translator's Glossary

ANIMAL (*dud 'gro*): see **six realms**.

APPEARANCE (*snang ba*): the shining forth of phenomena. Appearance of phenomena and the emptiness of inherent or concrete existence are to be seen not as contradictory, but as mutually compatible, a union.

ARHAT (*dgra bcom pa*): literally, one who has destroyed the foe; one who has overcome the internal enemy of ignorance and the afflictive emotions which are induced by ignorance. An Arhat is one who has gone beyond the cycle of birth, ageing, sickness and death through practising the Hinayana (q.v.) path but has not reached the omniscient status of a Buddha.

ARYA (*'phags pa*): literally, a Superior; an individual in either Hinayana or Mahayana who has reached the level of the path of seeing, that is to say, has attained direct realization of the truth but has not necessarily completed the path of training.

BLISS (*bde ba*): of the many levels of physical and mental bliss, this text primarily uses the term to refer to the very subtle pleasurable consciousness that, at the same time, is the most profound wisdom.

BREAKTHROUGH (*khregs chod*): the process of penetrating the profound reality of essential purity, the fact that all phenomena are from the start devoid of the misconceptions of inherent existence.

BUDDHA LINEAGE (*sangs rgyas kyi rigs*): the empty and clear nature of the mind that allows for the development of manifest Buddhahood. Lineage, here, has the sense of a necessary condition, this being the very nature of the mind.

CALM ABIDING (*zhi gnas*): a deep meditative state in which all distractions have been calmed and the mind is capable of abiding one-pointedly and joyously on any object.

CENTRAL CHANNEL (*rtsa dbu ma*): a channel which is said to range from the top of the head (or middle of the brow) to the base of the spine (or tip of the sexual organ) through which courses an essential fluid, referred to as 'drops'. It is flanked by channels on both sides which, in normal psychic life, constrict it and prevent movement of the impelling energies (called 'winds') inside it. The level of consciousness is determined by the movement of the fluid and energies, and thus a yogi seeks to control this process by meditative focusing and other techniques.

CLARITY (*gsal ba*): the basic luminous nature of the mind.

CLEAR LIGHT (*'od gsal*): the fundamental mind of clear light is the most basic level of consciousness. For ordinary persons, it manifests only at the time of death. A yogi seeks to actualize this basic, non-conceptual level of consciousness during his lifetime and to view all phenomena as manifestations of it.

COMPASSION (*snying rje*): the wish that all sentient beings be free of suffering, involving in its highest form the intention to bring such about through one's own efforts. The term is also used to indicate a bliss consciousness as well as the unimpeded nature of the mind which allows for spontaneous compassionate activity.

COMPLETE ENJOYMENT BODY: see **Three Bodies**.

COPPER-COLOURED MOUNTAIN (*zangs mdog dpal ri*): the legendary home of Padmasambhava, the root guru of the Nying-ma tradition.

CUTTING ATTACHMENT (*gcod*): the practice of internal exorcism, ridding oneself of control by the demon-like states of misconception and so forth.

CYCLIC EXISTENCE (*'khor ba*): the cycle of birth, ageing, sickness, and death repeated over and over again, without beginning but with an end for individuals when they achieve nirvana. Rebirth occurs in any of the six realms (q.v.).

DAKINI (*mkha' 'gro ma*): a very special type of female being who is capable of flying through space in her efforts to be of assistance, especially to tantric yogis. More subtly the dakini is the practitioner's link to a reality which is spacious and full of dharmic potentialities. The femininity of the dakini is linked with the symbolism of space or sky, the ability to give birth or to actualize the full range of expansive potentialities.

DELUSION/IGNORANCE (*gti mug/ma rig pa*): the absence of knowledge of the true reality as well as the active misconception of the nature of things as if they exist in their own right whereas they do not.

DEMI-GOD (*lha ma yin*): see **six realms**.

DEPENDENT-ARISING (*rten 'byung*): the profound principle of the conditioned origination of phenomena. It refers to the fact that products arise in dependence upon causes and conditions and that all phenomena – both products and non-products (such as space) – exist in dependence upon their parts and in dependence upon a conceptual consciousness that designates them. It is because of being dependent-arisings that it is said that all phenomena are empty of existing in their own right.

DESIRE (*'dod chags*): an attachment to remaining with a particular object.

DESIRE REALM (*'dod khams*): the realm of beings who are in general characterized as having sensuous desire and thus a distracted mind. The realms of humans are included here.

DOCTRINE (*chos*): not just the teachings or verbal doctrine (*lung gi chos*) but also the spiritual consciousnesses and cessations of suffering attained through those consciousnesses, called the realizational doctrine (*rtogs pa'i chos*).

DOUBLE SUFFERING (*sdug bsngal gyi sdug bsngal*): a double dose of suffering as when one thing goes wrong and then another. In other contexts, however, this term refers to the suffering of what is commonly recognized as physical or mental pain, double or not, as opposed to the more difficult to recognize forms of suffering, those of change and of conditioning (q.v.).

DROP (*thig le*): the essential fluid that courses in the channels governing levels of consciousness (see **central channel**), as well as visionary experiences of drops of various-coloured lights.

EFFECT SIMILAR TO THE CAUSE (*rgyu mthun gyi 'bras bu*): undergoing as a result of a former action a repetition of the same deed, such as murder, either as the perpetrator again or as the object – in this example, the victim of murder.

EMANATION BODY (*sprul pa'i sku*): see **Three Bodies**.

EMPOWERING BLESSING (*sbyin rlabs*): more literally, wave of magnificence; a heightening of body, speech, and mind through being affected by the powerful magnificence of the lama's or deity's exalted body, speech, and mind.

ENJOYMENT BODY (*longs spyod rdzogs pa'i sku*): see **Three Bodies**.

ENTITY (*ngo bo*): the basic clear entity or nature of the mind.

EQUALIZING AND SWITCHING SELF AND OTHER (*bdag gzhan mnyam brje*): a practice transmitted by Shantideva for the sake of developing an altruistic intention to become a Buddha. It revolves around recognizing the common or equal wish of all to be happy and to avoid suffering and then switching from self-cherishing to cherishing others.

EQUANIMITY (*btang snyoms*): a sense of even-mindedness towards all beings which is devoid of desire and hatred but definitely not indifferent.

ESSENTIAL PURITY (*ka dag/ka nas dag pa*): the natural emptiness of the mind which is realized through the breakthrough practices of the Great Perfection. *Ka* is the first letter of the Tibetan alphabet; thus, the term could be translated as 'purity from the letter *ka*', that is to say, from the beginning or from the very nature of things.

EXCITEMENT (*rgod pa*): the fault of the mind's scattering to desired objects when attempting to meditate.

EXPANSE/OPENNESS (*dbyings/klong*): the empty nature of things that is not a mere negation but is full of potentiality.

FIELD OF ASSEMBLY (*tshogs zhing*): the field of exalted objects with respect to which one can accumulate vast merit by making offering and so forth.

FORM BODY (*gzugs sku*): see **Three Bodies**.

FORM REALM (*gzugs khams*): a realm of existence above the desire realm, the latter being where our habitat is included. It is envisioned as being above the earth in space and having four levels corresponding to four degrees of concentration. Rebirth in the form realm is brought about by cultivating those concentrations while in this realm. Thus the term refers both to a place of rebirth and to a heightened degree of concentration surpassing even that of calm abiding (q.v.).

FORMLESS REALM (*gzugs med khams*): the highest realm within cyclic existence, constituted of four immaterial levels – infinite space, infinite consciousness, nothingness and peak of cyclic existence. These are both levels of rebirth as an immaterial being and levels of meditation that can be achieved during this life.

FORTUNATE REALMS (*bde 'gro*): literally, happy goings or travellings. See **six realms**.

FOUR BODIES (*sku bzhi*): see **Three Bodies**.

FOUR IMMEASURABLES (*tshad med bzhi*): equanimity (a sense of even-mindedness toward all beings), love (a wish that all beings have happiness and the causes of happiness), compassion (a wish that all beings be free from suffering and the causes of suffering), and joy (delight in the happiness and prosperity of beings). These attitudes are immeasurable because cultivating them accumulates immeasurable merit and because of being cultivated with respect to innumerable beings.

FOUR REVERSALS (*blo ldog rnam pa bzhi*): the four practices of realizing (i) the preciousness of human existence, (ii) the impermanence of life, (iii) the flaws in all forms of cyclic existence, and (iv) the inevitable relationship between good and bad actions and, respectively, pleasurable and painful effects. The first two reverse or turn the mind away from attachment to this life, and the latter two turn the mind away from attachment to future lives within the round of birth, ageing, sickness and death.

GENERATION OF THE ALTRUISTIC ASPIRATION (*sems bskyed*): the meditational process of generating an intention to become a Buddha in order to be of service to all beings. The term also refers to the mind of the intention to become enlightened itself. Such altruism is the basic motivation of Mahayana practice.

GOD (*lha*): see **six realms**.

GROUND (*sa*): one of the ten levels (*bhūmi*) of Bodhisattvas as they progress toward the supreme enlightenment of a Buddha. The non-conceptual wisdom consciousness realizing emptiness is called a ground in the sense that it gives rise to varying levels of qualities of body, speech, and mind as the Bodhisattva progresses, much as the earth serves as the basis for all that grows.

GURU: a Sanskrit term which literally means 'heavy' in the sense of being a person heavy with good qualities.

GURU YOGA (*bla ma'i rnal 'byor*): the meditational practice of devotion and worship of one's guru as a Buddha. Its prime intention is to cause one to become devoted to an ideal being, thereby mixing one's mind with an ideal state and thereby becoming closer to it.

HEARER (*nyan thos*): A *Shrāvaka*, a type of Hinayana practitioner who is known for *hearing* the doctrine, practising it, achieving the sought-after result and then causing others to *hear* that the result has been achieved. Hearers, who primarily seek their own liberation from cyclic existence, are to be distinguished from Bodhisattvas, who heroically intend to achieve full enlightenment or Buddhahood altruistically, so that they can most effectively help other beings.

HELL-BEING (*dmyal ba pa*): see **six realms.**

HIGH STATUS (*mngon mtho*): an elevated type of life within cyclic existence, specifically as a human, god, or demi-god. Within cyclic existence these types of beings are considered more fortunate than the others (animals, hungry ghosts, and hellbeings) but still caught within a diseased process. High status is in contrast with definite goodness (*nges legs*), a sure state of happiness on the level of complete liberation from cyclic existence or, even higher, Buddhahood itself.

HIGHEST YOGA TANTRA (*rnal 'byor bla med kyi rgyud*): also called Highest Yoga Mantra, this is the fourth and most advanced division of tantric practice. It has two divisions, a stage of generation in which the yogi imitates the process of death and in imagination emerges as a deity (an ideal being, whose very physical appearance is a manifestation of a union of compassion and realization of reality) and a stage of completion in which the yogi actually brings about a state like that of death and appears as a deity.

HINAYANA (*theg dman*): the Lower Vehicle or system of practices which can carry one, like a vehicle, to a state of liberation from cyclic existence but which, unlike the Mahayana or Great Vehicle, cannot carry one by means of its practices to Buddhahood. The ethical codes of monks and nuns is Hinayana, and thus, although it is lower than the Mahayana, it is neither despised nor shunned.

HUMAN (*mi*): see **six realms.**

HUNGRY GHOST (*yi dvags*): see **six realms.**

INHERENT EXISTENCE (*rang bzhin gyis grub pa*): existence by way of the object's own being, existence in the object's own right. Such existence never did or will occur, but beings conceive that persons and other phenomena exist this way and thereby are drawn into desire and hatred as well as other afflictive emotions. Through these falsely based states of mind, actions are committed which result in further entrapment within the round of suffering.

Realizing the absence of inherent existence acts as the antidote to its misconception.

INITIATION (*dbang*): the empowerment or authorization of a person to practise visualization of oneself as a deity and so forth in tantra.

INTERMEDIATE AEON (*bar bskal*): a great aeon is composed of eighty intermediate aeons, which are divided into four groups with twenty each for the period of formation of a world system, its duration, destruction and vacuity.

INTROSPECTION (*shes bzhin*): the factor of a meditating consciousness that performs occasional inspection of the mind to determine whether laxity or excitement have arisen or are about to arise.

KNOWLEDGE BEARER (*rig 'dzin*): special beings who have attained high levels of tantric practice, named from the point of view of their having knowledge of reality.

LAMA (*bla ma*): a guru (q.v.).

LEAP-OVER (*thod rgal*): the meditative practice that unleashes the spontaneous nature of the mind, so called because it involves a skipping or different order of certain levels of training.

LIVING BEING (*'gro ba*): literally, a traveller; a being who travels or moves about among the levels of cyclic existence like a bee caught in a jar. See **six realms**.

MAHAYANA (*theg chen*): the Great Vehicle, so named because of being a system of practice that can carry one, like a vehicle, through to full Buddhahood at which time one can, again like a vehicle, bear or carry the task of supporting the welfare of all beings. It is contrasted to the Hinayana which is capable of bringing one only to one's own liberation and thus not capable of bringing about the full development of body, speech, and mind. Though contrasted with Hinayana, it is not antithetical to Hinayana, for it represents a higher level of spiritual progress, built on the lower.

MEDITATIVE STABILIZATION (*ting nge 'dzin*): a high level of concentration (*samādhi*) achieved through eliminating distraction both to external objects such as those of desire and to internal states of laxity and lethargy.

MENTAL CONTINUUM (*rgyud*): the stream of consciousness in the sense of one moment of consciousness generating another, like the continuum of a flame.

MERIT/MERITORIOUS POWER (*bsod nams*): the mental force accumulated through healthy actions of body, speech and mind. Merit and its opposite, sin (not to be confused with sin against God), are the stuff of the universe in the sense that everything, both internal and external, is created by this power, acting collectively in the case of the environment and individually in the case of one's body, for instance.

MIND-BASIS-OF-ALL (*kun gzhi rnam shes*): in the Mind-Only (*Chittamātra*) school which follows the teachings of the Indian sage Asanga, this is the consciousness that serves as the foundation of all of cyclic existence and of nirvana, in other words, the low and the sublime. In it the seeds or potencies which produce the appearance of the world and the beings within it are infused, like imprints, by one's own actions; later these are activated by conditions and manifest as various appearances, pleasure, pain, and so forth. The term is also used here to refer to a basic level of consciousness.

MIND OF ENLIGHTENMENT (*byang chub kyi sems*): this does not refer to an enlightened mind but to the intention to become enlightened as well as a Bodhisattva's direct realization of reality. The first is the conventional mind of enlightenment, and the second, the ultimate mind of enlightenment. It is *of* enlightenment in the sense of being toward enlightenment.

MINDFULNESS (*dran pa*): here, the meditative factor of not forgetting one's object of observation. It and introspection are the essential ingredients for attaining deep meditative states.

NATURE BODY (*ngo bo nyid sku*): see **Three Bodies**.

NECTAR (*bdud rtsi*): the drink of deathlessness (*amrta*), imagined as a fluid that confers freedom from the realm of birth and death and often imagined in meditations concerned with purifying defilements.

NON-CONCEPTUAL (*rtog med*): a consciousness which contacts its object directly, without the medium of internal images or constructs.

OBSTRUCTION (*sgrib pa*): there are basically two types of obstructions, those preventing liberation from the cycle of suffering, called afflictive obstructions (*nyon sgrib*), and those preventing omniscience, called the obstructions to objects of knowledge (*shes bya'i sgrib pa*), or, as often translated here, obstructions to omniscience. The practices of the path are aimed at removing these obstacles – the Hinayana or Low Vehicle being capable of removing the obstructions to liberation, and the Mahayana or Great Vehicle being required for removing the obstructions to omniscience.

PERFECTION (*pha rol tu phyin pa*): the six virtues of giving, ethics, patience, effort, concentration and wisdom are present in their perfected form only in Buddhas. However as means for reaching perfection, they are also present in Bodhisattvas. The word may also be translated as 'transcendence', gone beyond.

PERSONAL DEITY (*yi dam*): a supramundane being, a deity who both protects the holy and serves as a meditational model so that the yogi may meditate on himself in this form, thereby gaining **siddhis** (q.v.), feats or special powers.

PREDISPOSITION (*bag chags*): a potency deposited in the mind, much like an imprint, by an action of body, speech, or mind. It can be activated by favourable conditions, producing pleasure, pain, and so forth in accordance with the nature of the original deed.

PURE LAND (*dag zhing*): a land emanated by a Buddha either for a Complete Enjoyment Body or an Emanation Body to teach doctrine to fortunate beings. It arises through the force of aspirations and practices done while one is a Bodhisattva and serves as a medium through which beings, who are not yet Buddhas, can meet enlightened beings in a very special environment. Practitioners are often advised to view even the present land as a pure land, constructed from the fusion of compassion and wisdom, as a preparation for seeing the world without the overlay of ordinary perception.

QUINTESSENTIAL INSTRUCTION (*man ngag*): a distillation of important teachings so that their essence is more easily grasped.

SAMANTABHADRA (*kun tu bzang po*): the basic Buddha, often identified with the Truth Body itself; also, a Bodhisattva known especially for his aspirational prayers for the well-being of all living creatures. The term can also refer to the 'all good' basic nature of the mind.

SEAL (*phyag rgya*): a gesture with the hands to symbolize such things as objects of offering, flowers and so forth. Also, a female consort who serves to induce the great bliss consciousness is called a seal because when the great bliss consciousness realizes emptiness, all phenomena appear as the sport of that consciousness and thus are imprinted with the seal or stamp of bliss.

SECRET MANTRA VEHICLE (*gsang sngags kyi theg pa*): the Mantrayana or Tantrayana, as distinguished from Sutrayana. It is secret because it is not suitable to be revealed to those who are not fit vessels for it, that is, for those whose minds have not been prepared by the preliminary practices. Mantra means protection (*trā*) of the mind (*man*) in the sense of visualizing one's body, speech and mind as well as environment and activities as pure, and thus keeping one's mind from ordinary appearances and a consequent conception of ordinariness.

SENTIENT BEING (*sems can*): beings with minds that have obstructions yet to be removed. Thus a Buddha is not a sentient being, though everyone else is.

SIDDHI (*dngos grub*): a special feat or power attained through yogic practice, usually through the process of visualizing a deity, either in front of oneself or imagining oneself as a deity, and thereby coming closer to the state of the deity, after which the feat is as if bestowed by the deity. The supreme siddhi is Buddhahood itself, whereas common siddhis range from flying through the air, or lengthening the life span, to understanding treatises immediately upon reading them, to pacifying illness, etc. The Tibetan word would be translated literally as 'actual accomplishment', so called because through imagination one brings the feat into reality.

SIN (*sdig pa*): not an offence against God, but an unhealthy action of body, speech, or mind that by its own nature will result in suffering.

SIX REALMS (*'gro ba rigs drug*): literally, the six types of travellers or the living beings who travel from station to station within the cycle of rebirth. The six are divided into two groups; fortunate and unfortunate beings. Fortunate beings (*bde 'gro*, literally, happy travellings) are the three: humans, demi-gods, and gods. Rebirth in these three ways occurs due to a virtuous action in an earlier lifetime. Human life is particularly suited for religious practice because of having a mixture of pleasure and pain, neither being so overpowering as to make the thought of practice impossible. Demi-gods have greater resources than humans but are particularly afflicted with jealousy of the still more prosperous and long-lived gods.

Unfortunate beings (*ngan 'gro*, literally, bad travellings) are the three: animals, hungry ghosts, and hell-beings. Animals are particularly afflicted with dullness and are excessively used for others' purposes. Hungry ghosts are smitten with hunger and thirst, and hell-beings are mostly tortured with either heat or cold. One is said to be reborn as an animal due to actions of delusion or stupidity, as a hungry ghost from excessive desire, and as a hell-being from hatred.

It is important to imagine these six realms vividly, as these represent tendencies in our own minds; having imagined them, the various acts of charity and so forth as well as reflection on the emptiness of inherent existence will be extended into these levels of the personality. Yogic practice is thereby made more powerful and more integrative.

SKY GOER: see **dakini**.

SOLITARY REALIZER (*rang sangs rgyas/rang rgyal*): a type of Hinayana practitioner noted for finishing the practices for achieving his level of nirvana without depending on a teacher in his last lifetime. Though in earlier lifetimes a Solitary Realizer relies on teachers, in his last lifetime within the cycle of rebirth he achieves realization alone.

SPACE-LIKE MEDITATIVE EQUIPOISE (*mnyam bzhag nam mkha' lta bu*): the meditative state in which just emptiness is perceived – nothing else appears. Just as space is merely the absence of obstructive contact, so emptiness is the mere absence of inherent existence; thus the meditative realization of emptiness is said to be space-like. The fact that conventional objects do not appear in this state does not however mean that nothing exists; rather, the yogi is focusing on the analytical unfindability of objects, not paying attention to conventional appearances.

STAGE OF COMPLETION (*rdzogs rim*): see **Secret Mantra Vehicle**.

STAGE OF GENERATION (*skyed rim*): see **Secret Mantra Vehicle**.

SUFFERING OF CHANGE (*'gyur ba'i sdug bsngal*): all pleasure that is contaminated with the sense of inherent existence is considered to be a suffering of change because it so easily turns into pain, showing that it does not have a basic nature of pleasure.

SUFFERING OF CONDITIONING (*'du byed kyi sdug bsngal*): even neutral feelings are considered to be this type of suffering because of being involved in a general process that is subject to afflictive emotions and actions motivated by them. Though these are not painful on the surface, one is trapped within a condition of pain.

THREE BODIES (*sku gsum*): a Buddha's physical and mental aspects are summarized in the Three Bodies – Truth, Complete Enjoyment, and Emanation. The Truth Body is a Buddha's omniscient consciousness and its emptiness of inherent existence; it is called 'Truth' in the sense that it is the highest form of true paths as an omniscient consciousness and of true cessations as the complete cessation of all obstructions. The Complete Enjoyment Body is an ideal manifestation in form of the Truth Body for the sake of preaching to advanced trainees in **pure lands** (q.v.). Emanation Bodies are other physical manifestations, in subtle or coarse form, emitted by the Complete Enjoyment Body, again for the sake of aiding sentient beings.

When the Truth Body is considered in its two aspects, as omniscient consciousness (or Wisdom Truth Body) and as the emptiness of that consciousness (or Nature Body), it can be said that a Buddha has Four Bodies. Again, when the Complete Enjoyment and Emanation Bodies are considered under the single rubric of being form, it can be said that a Buddha has Two Bodies – Form and Truth Bodies.

THREE JEWELS (*dkon mchog gsum*): Buddha as the teacher of refuge, the Doctrine as the actual refuge, and the Spiritual Community as helpers towards that refuge. They are called 'Jewels' because their appearance in the world is rare, they are undefiled, powerful, the ornament of the world, superior, and changeless.

THREE VEHICLES (*theg pa gsum*): see **Hinayana**, **Mahayana**, and **Secret Mantra Vehicle**.

TRUTH BODY (*chos sku*): see **Three Bodies**.

UNFORTUNATE REALMS (*ngan 'gro*): literally, bad destinations. See **six realms**.

WIND (*rlung*): inner currents of air (or energy) that control physical functions and serve as the bases or mounts of consciousness; it is said that consciousness is mounted on wind like a rider on a horse.

WISDOM (*shes rab/ye shes*): a developed form of consciousness that in its ultimate form realizes the nature of phenomena and in its conventional form distinguishes appearances.

YOUTHFUL ENCASED BODY (*gzhon nu bum pa'i sku*): a special type of body achieved by an adept that is still encased or contained within the ordinary body. It is reminiscent of the illusory body in the Guhyasamaja system, though in the case of a pure illusory body it is the yogi's voluntary choice to return inside the ordinary body; here, some defilements still need to be removed. At times, the text also seems to refer to this as a fully developed Buddha body.

Bibliography

Entries in the Tibetan Tripitaka Research Foundation Publication of the *Tibetan Tripitaka* (Tokyo-Kyoto, 1956) are indicated by the letter *P*, standing for 'Peking edition'.

1 SUTRAS

Condensed Perfection of Wisdom Sutra
Sañchayagāthāprajñāpāramitāsūtra
Shes rab kyi pha rol tu phyin pa sdud pa tshigs su bcad pa
P735, Vol.21

Sutra of the Wise Man and the Fool
Damamūkanāmasūtra
mDzangs blun zhes bya ba'i mdo
P1008, Vol.40

2 OTHER WORKS

Ba-drul Jik-may-chö-gi-wang-bo (dPal-sprul 'Jigs-med-chos-kyi-dbang-po), born 1808. *Instructions on the Preliminaries to the Great Perfection Teaching Called 'Heart Essence of Vast Openness', the Sacred Word of Lama Gun-sang.*
rDzogs pa chen po klong chen snying tig gi sngon 'gro'i khrid yig kun bzang bla ma'i zhal lung
Rum-theg: Karma'i chos-sgar, 1968

Cha-har Ge-shay (Cha-har dGe-bshes bLo-bzang-tshul-khrims), eighteenth century. *Commentary on the Ye Dharma*

Bibliography 229

Ye dharma'i 'grel pa
The Collected Works of Cha-har Dge-bśes, Vol.1
New Delhi: Chatring Jansar Tenzin, 1973

Jik-may-ling-ba ('Jigs-med-gling-pa Rang-byung-rdo-rje), 1729/30–1798. *Recitation of the Preliminaries to the Heart Essence of Vast Openness, Illuminating the Good Path to Omniscience*
kLong chen snying tig gi sngon 'gro'i ngag 'don rnam mkhyen lam bzang gsal byed, (as found in) kLong chen snying thig
n.p., 1970

Long-chen-rap-jam (kLong-chen-pa Dri-med-'od'zer), 1308–63. *Precious Treasury of the Supreme Vehicle*
Theg pa'i mchog rin po che'i mdzod
Gangtok, Dodrup Chen Rinpoche, 1969[?]

Long-chen-rap-jam. *Treasury of Tenets, Illuminating the Meaning of All Vehicles*
Theg pa mtha' dag gi don gsal bar byed pa grub pa'i mtha' rin po che'i mdzod
Gangtok: Dodrup Chen Rinpoche, 1969[?]

Nāgārjuna (kLu-sgrub). *Friendly Letter*
Suhṛllekha
bShes pa'i spring yig
P5682, Vol.129

Nga-wang-bel-sang (Ngag-dbang-dpal-bzang), 1879–1941. *Notes on the Sacred Word of Lama Gun-sang*
rDzogs pa chen po klong chen snying thig gi sngon 'gro'i khrid yig kun bzang bla ma'i zhal lung gi zin bris
sPang-dgon [?], 1969 [?]

Shāntideva (Zhi-ba-lha). *Engaging in the Bodhisattva Deeds*
Bodhisattvacharyāvatāra
Byang chub sems dpa'i spyod pa la 'jug pa
P5272, Vol.99

Notes

1. kLong-chen-pa Dri-med-'od-zer, *Precious Treasury of the Supreme Vehicle (Theg pa'i mchog rin po che'i mdzod)* (Gangtok: Dodrup Chen Rinpoche, 1969 [?]). The other references in this paragraph are to the same author's *Treasury of Tenets, Illuminating the Meaning of All Vehicles (Theg pa mtha' dag gi don gsal bar byed pa grub pa'i mtha' rin po che'i mdzod)* (Gangtok, Dodrup Chen Rinpoche, 1969 [?]); dPal-sprul 'Jigs-med-chos-kyi-dbang-po's, *Instructions on the Preliminaries to the Great Perfection Teaching Called 'Heart Essence of Vast Openness', the Sacred Word of Lama Gun-sang (rDzogs pa chen po klong chen snying tig gi sngon 'gro'i khrid yig kun bzang bla ma'i zhal lung)* (Rum-theg, Karma'i-chos-sgar, 1968; also Paro, Ngodup, 1976) abbreviated in later notes as *Gun-sang*; and Ngag-dbang-dpal-bzang's *Notes on the Sacred Word of Lama Gun-sang (rDzogs pa chen po klong chen snying tig gi sngon 'gro'i khrid yig kun bzang bla ma'i zhal lung gi zin bris)*, (sPang-dgon [?], 1969 [?], abbreviated henceforth as '*Notes*.'
2. 'A Standard System of Tibetan Transcription,' HJAS, Vol.22, pp.261–7, 1959.
3. Wisdom Publications, 1983, at the beginning.
4. The remainder of the Introduction is a commentary on *Gun-sang* 2.1–4.3 (all citations are from the Rum-theg edition).
5. The text reads *rje btsun*, which is being interpreted as *dpal ldan*, glorious (*shrīman*).
6. In Tibetan these are *snang nyams, stong nyams, bde nyams*.
7. Chapter 2 correlates with *Gun-sang* 4.3–10.3 and *Notes* 9a.5–23b.2. The common external practices are so called because of being common objects of contemplation in all vehicles (*Notes* 102.5).
8. Chapter 3 correlates with *Gun-sang* 10.3–22.5 and *Notes* 23b.2–26a.6.
9. Chapter 4 correlates with *Gun-sang* 22.5–50.4 and *Notes* 26b.1–39b.2.
10. Chapter 5 correlates with *Gun-sang* 50.4–84.6 and *Notes* 39b.2–44b.6.

11. Nagarjuna's *Friendly Letter*.
12. Chapter 6 correlates with *Gun-sang* 85.1–104.3 and *Notes* 44b.6–53b.2; the latter is a broader treatment of the topic.
13. Nagarjuna's *Friendly Letter*.
14. Chapter 7 correlates with *Gun-sang* 104.3–150.4 and *Notes* 44b.6–53b.2 (as did Chapter 6).
15. Chapter 8 correlates with *Gun-sang* 150.4–203.5 and *Notes* 53b.2–59a.5.
16. *Engaging in the Bodhisattva Deeds (Bodhisattvacharyāvatāra)*, v.16.
17. *dGe-bshes 'Ban*.
18. The Tibetan name is *Pha-dam-pa-sangs-rgyas*, whom some identify as Bodhidharma.
19. Chapter 9 correlates with *Gun-sang* 203.6–257.5 and *Notes* 59a.5–63b.1.
20. Chapter 10 correlates with *Gun-sang* 257.5–294.1 and *Notes* 63b.2–93a.1.
21. The bracketed material is taken from *Notes* 67b.3 and 67a.5.
22. Chapter 11 correlates with *Gun-sang* 294.2–409.5 and *Notes* 93a.1–158b.6.
23. *Engaging in the Bodhisattva Deeds*, v.80.
24. *lCags-shing-pa*.
25. Chapter 12 correlates with *Gun-sang* 409.5–436.6 and *Notes* 158b.6–167a.5.
26. See Nagarjuna's *Friendly Letter*, stanza 14.
27. The king was Ajātashatru.
28. *Engaging in the Bodhisattva Deeds* I.13.
29. The translation of the mantra together with the word by word explanation has been drawn by the translator from a commentary by Si-du (*Si-tu*) Paṇ-chen (*Yi ge brgya pa'i don dang bklag thabs bcas nyung bsdus su bkod pa*) a handwritten copy of which was graciously provided by Geshe Dawa Sangbo. With respect to Vajrasattva's pledge, Nga-wang-bel-sang's *Notes* (162a.3) say, 'Earlier on a path of learning, Vajrasattva [made the pledge], "In the future may all the sins and infractions of all those who hold merely my name be purified! If not, may I not become enlightened."'
30. Chapter 13 correlates with *Gun-sang* 437.1–456.6 and *Notes* 167a.5–174a.5.
31. These refer not to the seminal essence but to drops of light that are seen on a stage of the path.
32. Chapter 14 correlates with *Gun-sang* 457.1–473.1 and *Notes* 174a.5–180b.5.
33. Chapter 15 correlates with *Gun-sang* 473.2–532.1 and *Notes* 180b.2–200b.3.

34. Part Three has been translated and edited from Khetsun Sangpo Rinbochay's oral commentary on Long-chen-rap-jam's *Treasury of the Supreme Vehicle (Theg mchog mdzod)*.

35. This prose section before the recitation text has been added from Khetsun Sangpo Rinbochay's oral teachings. The remainder of Part Four is a translation of *Recitation of the Preliminaries to the Heart Essence of Vast Openness, Illuminating the Good Path to Omniscience (kLong chen snying tig gi sngon 'gro ngag, don rnam mkhyen lam bzang gsal byed)* by Jik-may-ling-ba *('Jigs-med-gling-pa)*. The edition used is that found in *kLong chen snying thig* (n.p., 1970).

36. The translation of the mantra and the bracketed additions are based on Cha-har Ge-shay's *Commentary on the Ye Dharma (Ye dharma'i 'grel pa)* The Collected Works of Cha-har Dge-bśes, Vol.1 (New Delhi: Chatring Jansar Tenzin, 1973, pp.569–74).

37. The phrase, 'The lama knows,' is an expression of complete faith and confidence in the lama in the sense of putting oneself in the care of another who knows everything needed in one's particular situation. It is called 'the faith of "you know"' *(khyed shes kyi dad pa)*, or, less literally, 'the faith of entrustment'.

38. See note 21.

39. See note 31.

40. In accordance with a suggestion from Khetsun Sangpo Rinbochay, a section of fifteen lines of poetry (in translation) has been moved from here to the end of the next prose section. Similarly, a long petition of the lineage of lamas which appeared after Padmasambhava's mantra has been moved to a separate section following the conclusion of inititation. The text as amended accords with the ordering of *The Sacred Word of Lama Gun-sang*.

41. The master is Tri-song-de-dzen *(Khri-srong-lde-brtsan,* born 742); the deputies are twenty-five of his governmental ministers who became disciples of Padmasambhava; the friend is Ye-shay-tso-gyel, Padmasambhava's consort.

42. The four Knowledge Bearers constitute a division of attainments from the path of accumulation to the actualization of Buddhahood; they are the fruition, power over life, seal, and spontaneous Knowledge Bearers.

Index

Made in the USA
Columbia, SC
10 October 2022

69221642R00145